A-level
Psychology
Revision Guide
For The
Edexcel
2015 Specification

Year 2

Clinical Psychology
Criminological Psychology
Issues and Debates
Research Methods

Faye Carlisle

Text Copyright @ 2016 Faye C Carlisle
All Right Reserved

Contents

Introduction 9

Chapter 1-Clinical Psychology 15

Diagnosis of mental disorders with reference to deviance, dysfunction, distress and danger 15

Diagnostic systems: DSM V and ICD for mental health 16

Reliability of diagnoses in relation to diagnostic systems 16

Validity of diagnoses in relation to diagnostic systems 17

The symptoms and features of schizophrenia, including thought insertion, hallucinations, delusions, disordered thinking 18

The function of neurotransmitters as an explanation for schizophrenia 19

The genetic explanation of schizophrenia 20

The cognitive explanation of schizophrenia 21

Drug therapy as a treatment for schizophrenia 22

Cognitive behavioural therapy (CBT) for schizophrenia. 23

The features and symptoms of anorexia nervosa. 24

The genetic explanation of anorexia nervosa. 24

Social learning theory as an explanation of anorexia nervosa. 25

Drug therapy as a treatment for anorexia nervosa. 26

Rational Emotive Therapy (RET) for anorexia nervosa 26

Cultural effects and mental health disorders 27

Health and Care Professions Council (HCPC) guidelines for clinical practitioners ... 29

Longitudinal methods in mental health research. 29

Cross-sectional research in mental health. 29

Meta-analyses in mental health research. 30

Primary and secondary data 30

Case studies 31

Lavarenne et al. (2013) Containing psychotic patients with fragile boundaries: a single group case study. 31

Interviews in clinical psychology. 32

An example of an interview: Vallentine et al. (2010) Psycho-educational group for detained offender patients: understanding mental illness. 33

Measures of central tendency 34

Measures of Dispersion	35
Level of significance	37
Chi-square test	38
Spearman's Rho test	40
Wilcoxon Signed Rank test	41
Mann-Whitney U test	43
Thematic analysis	45
Grounded theory.	46
Rosenhan (1973) On being sane in insane places	47
Carlsson et al. (1999) Network interactions in schizophrenia – therapeutic implications.	48
Guardia et al. (2012) Imagining One's Own and Someone Else's Body Actions: Dissociation in Anorexia Nervosa.	49
Key question 'How are mental health issues portrayed in the media?'	50
Example practical: A content analysis that explores attitudes to mental health	51
Ethical issues in clinical psychology	52
Practical issues in the design and implementation of research	52
Reductionism and clinical psychology	52
Comparing different factors/themes used to explain mental disorder	52
Clinical psychology as a science	52
Cultural issues in clinical psychology	52
The nature-nurture debate in clinical psychology	53
Psychological knowledge over time in clinical psychology	53
Issues of social control in clinical psychology	53
The use of clinical psychological knowledge in society	53
Socially sensitive research and clinical psychology	53
Exemplar exam question in Clinical Psychology.	55
Chapter 2-Criminological Psychology	**58**
Brain injury as a biological explanation of criminal behaviour	58
The amygdala as a biological explanation of aggressive behaviour	59
XYY syndrome as a biological explanation of criminal and anti-social behaviour	59
Labelling and the self-fulfilling prophecy as a social explanation of criminal and anti-social behaviour	60

- The cognitive interview 61
- Ethical interview techniques 61
- Psychological formulations 61
- Anger management 62
- Diet as a treatment for offenders 63
- Factors influencing eye-witness testimony, (including post-event information and weapon focus) 64
- Factors influencing jury decision-making, including characteristics of the defendant and pre-trial publicity 65
- Individual differences in criminal and anti-social behaviour 65
- Social learning theory and criminal/anti-social behaviour 66
- Biological causes for criminal/anti-social behaviour in relation to development 67
- Laboratory experiments and eye-witness effectiveness 67
- Field experiments and eye-witness effectiveness 68
- Case studies and eye-witness effectiveness 69
- Loftus and Palmer (1974) Reconstruction of automobile destruction: An example of the interaction between language and memory 70
- Valentine T and Mesout J (2009) Eyewitness identification under stress in the London Dungeon 72
- Key question: 'Is eye-witness testimony too unreliable to trust?' 73
- Example practical: The effect of leading questions on participant's responses 75
- Ethical issues in criminological psychology 77
- Practical issues in the design and implementation of research 77
- Reductionism in criminological psychology 77
- Comparing different ways of explaining criminal behaviour 78
- Criminological psychology as a science 78
- Cultural issues in criminological psychology 78
- Gender in criminological psychology 78
- The nature-nurture debate in criminological psychology 78
- How psychological understanding has developed over time in criminological psychology 79
- Psychological knowledge and criminological psychology 79
- Socially sensitive research in criminological psychology 79
- Issues of social control in criminological psychology 79

Exemplar exam question for criminological psychology 80

Chapter 3-Issues and debates 83
The Nature-Nurture Debate.. 83
The debate over whether psychology a science 83
The debate over whether animals should be used in psychological research 84
Cultural issues in psychological research... 84
Cross-cultural research 84
Issues related to the use of psychological knowledge as a means of social control 85
Ethical Issues in psychological research with humans............................... 85
Ethical Issues in animal experiments 86
Ethics when researching obedience and prejudice in social psychology............ 86
Practical issues in the design and implementation of research in social psychology 87
Reductionism in social psychology 87
Comparisons between ways of explaining behaviour in social psychology 87
Social psychology as a science.. 88
Cultural issues in social psychology 88
Gender issues in social psychology 88
The nature-nurture debate in social psychology...................................... 88
Understanding of how psychological knowledge had developed over time in social psychology 88
Issues of social control in social psychology 89
The use of social psychological knowledge in society................................ 89
Issues related to socially sensitive research in social psychology.................. 89
Ethical issues in cognitive psychology... 89
Practical issues in the design and implementation of research in cognitive psychology 89
Reductionism in cognitive psychology 90
Comparing different explanations of memory in cognitive psychology 90
Cognitive psychology as a science 90
The nature nurture debate in cognitive psychology................................... 90
How psychological knowledge has developed over time in cognitive psychology.... 90
The use of psychological knowledge from the cognitive approach within society 91
Ethical issues in biological psychology... 91

Practical issues in the design and implementation of research in biological psychology 92

Reductionism in biological psychology 92

Biological psychology as a science 93

The nature-nurture debate in biological psychology 93

Understanding how biological psychological knowledge has developed over time .. 93

Issues of social control in biological psychology 93

The use of psychological knowledge from the biological approach 94

Issues related to socially sensitive research in biological psychology 94

Ethical issues related to learning theories 94

Practical issues in the design and implementation of research related to learning theories 94

Reductionism in relation to learning theories 95

Comparisons between different learning theories 95

Psychology as a science and learning theories 95

Cultural issues in relation to learning theories 95

Gender issues in relation to learning theories 95

The nature-nurture debate in the learning approach 96

How psychological knowledge had developed over time in relation to learning theories 96

Issues of social control in relation to learning theories 96

Learning theories and the use of psychological knowledge in society 96

Issues related to socially sensitive research in relation to learning theories 97

Exemplar exam question issues and debates 98

Chapter 4-Research Methods 101

Laboratory Experiments 101

Field experiments 101

Natural Experiments 101

Questionnaires 102

Observations 102

Interviews 104

Content analysis 104

Case Studies 105

Correlational Techniques	105
Thematic Analysis	106
Longitudinal Studies	106
Cross-sectional Studies	106
Meta-analyses	107
Quantitative and qualitative	107
Comparing research methods.	108
Exemplar exam question on research methods	109

Introduction

About this guide

This revision guide covers clinical psychology, criminological psychology, research methods and issues and debates. It includes descriptions of key studies, theories, treatments and example practicals. It also uses a clear system of evaluation throughout, which makes it easier to evaluate in the exam.

Edexcel Examination Structure

Paper 1 examines your knowledge of social psychology, cognitive psychology, biological psychology and learning theories. It includes questions on issues and debates related to these topics. Unit 1 is worth 35% of the marks for the whole A-level and is assessed in a 2 hour exam.

Paper 2 examines your knowledge clinical psychology and one of the following optional topic areas: Criminological psychology, Child psychology or Health psychology. This revision guide covers only one option: Criminological psychology. Paper 2 is worth 35% of the marks for the whole A-level and is assessed in a 2 hour exam.

Paper 3 examines psychological skills. Section A has 24 marks and covers the topic area of research methods. Section B has 24 marks asks questions on psychological studies from social psychology, cognitive psychology, biological psychology and learning theories. Section C has 32 marks and covers the topic area of issues and debates in psychology. Paper 3 is worth 30% of the marks for the whole A-level and is assessed in a 2 hour exam.

Note: Both paper 1 and paper 2 have 90 marks available so you have 1 minute 20 seconds for each mark. A 12 mark question should take you 16 minutes and a 16 mark question should take you 21 minutes so make sure you leave enough time to do the extended response questions.
Paper 3 has 80 marks available so you have 1 minute 30 seconds for each mark. A 20 mark extended response question should take you 30 minutes so it is important to plan for this.

Revision strategies

Complete sample or past exam papers and look at the mark schemes and examiners reports to see what the examiner wants.

Focus on what you find difficult to understand and get to grips with it.

Revise in 25 minutes chunks, with 5 minute breaks in the middle to keep your mind alert.

Do not just read this revision guide. Active revision is more effective: Make notes, draw mind maps, record audio clips and write revision cards.

Remember to revise methodology i.e. research methods, types of design, levels of data, inferential tests and any practicals you carried out. You will be able to gain lots of marks for understanding scientific procedures and techniques.

Assessment objectives (taken from Edexcel specification)

AO1-Demonstrate a knowledge and understanding of scientific ideas, processes, techniques and procedures
AO2-Apply knowledge and understanding of scientific ideas, processes, techniques and procedures
AO3-Analyse, interpret and evaluate scientific information, ideas and evidence

Evaluating Studies, Theories and Treatments

Studies

You can use GRAVE to help you evaluate a study.

Generalisability-How generalisable is the study? Are the participants in the sample representative of the wider population?

Reliability-How easy is the study to replicate and get similar results? If a study have a standardised procedure and was done under controlled conditions, then it is easy to replicate. A study is reliable if it has been replicated and similar results have been found.

Application to real life-Can the study explain real life events or be applied to real life situations.

Validity-Does the study have internal validity? Internal validity reflects on the experimenter's competence-The person who is doing the experiment's ability to carry out the study well. Was the experiment well-designed? Did any factors interfere with the experiment?

A study has **internal validity** when the material or procedures used in the research measured what they were supposed to measure. For example, in Milgram's experiment on obedience, participants had to giving increasing levels of electric shock to another person on the orders of an authority figure. The number of shocks the participants were prepared to give was a good indicator of their obedience level and so the study has construct validity (an indicator of internal validity).

Avoiding **demand characteristics** is important to ensure internal validity. Demand characteristics refer to when participants guess what a study is about and then change their behaviour. For example, a participant might guess that a study is on obedience and deliberately change their behaviour to show how easily people obey or to show how difficult it is to get people to obey.

A study has **experimental validity** if participants believe in the experimental situation. For example, in Milgram's study, if the participants believed they really were giving real electric shocks and thought that Mr. Wallace was another participant rather than a confederate, then the study has experimental validity (an indicator of internal validity).

If a study has predictive validity, then this is another indicator of internal validity. A study has **predictive validity** if it accurately predicts a result in the future. For example, if a person gains a high score on a test measuring racial prejudice and then engages in acts of discrimination, then the test has predictive validity.

Does the study have **external validity**? A study has external validity if the findings can be generalised to other situations and populations. If a study is done in participants' natural environment and involves a natural task that might be experienced in everyday life then it has **ecological validity**, which is an indicator of external validity.

Population validity relates to whether the sample can be generalised to the population it is meant to represent. For example, if you are looking at sixth form students' views on university tuition fees but only use a sample of private school students, then the sample lacks population validity. If a study has population validity then this is an indicator of external validity.

Ethics-Does the study have any ethical issues? Were participants protected from physical and psychological harm? Were participants given the right to withdraw? Did the participants give fully informed consent or were they deceived about any aspect of the study? Were the participants debriefed? Was the anonymity of the participants protected? Was the researcher competent to carry out the research?

You do not have to discuss all these points in your evaluation. For example, if there are no ethical issues then you don't need to discuss them. GRAVE is just a trigger to jog your memory and to help you evaluate.

You should also consider the objectivity and credibility of the research.

Objectivity- This refers to whether the study has collected data that is unbiased. Quantitative (numerical) data is likely to be impartial.

Credibility-This refers to whether the study is trustworthy. Research is more trustworthy if it is scientific, reliable, valid and unbiased.

Theories

You can use SEA to evaluate a theory.

Studies that support/contradict the theory. You can also make one evaluative point per study you use in your evaluation. Do not spend too long evaluating any studies as you have been asked to focus on evaluating the theory. Remember that a theory is someone's idea about how something works.

Explanation-What are the problems/limitations of the theory? Are there alternative explanations?

Application to real life-How can the study be applied to real life situations or events?

Treatments

You can use DESERT to help you evaluate a treatment.

Directive- Is the patient reliant on the therapist for all the answers? Is there a power imbalance? If the therapist has too much power then the treatment is directive.

Effectiveness-How effective is the therapy at treating the behaviour?

Side effects-Are there any side effects to the therapy?

Expense-How expensive is the therapy in terms of time and money?

Reasons-Does the therapy looks at the underlying causes/reasons for the behaviour?

Types of people-Does the therapy only work on certain types of people?

What level of detail should you give in an evaluation?

For a short-answer evaluation question, your answer should only contain evaluative points i.e. assume the examiner knows the material already.
However, when you have 8 or more marks for evaluating, then you are expected to give some description to set up your argument. For example, for an 8 mark question on evaluating a study, 4 marks are for describing those things that you are then going to evaluate i.e. if you are going to discuss generalisability, then you should talk about the sample and the population used. The other 4 marks are for evaluation.
For a 12 mark question, 6 marks are for showing knowledge and understanding and 6 marks are for evaluation.

Compare the following two answers:

Evaluate Milgram's basic study (4 marks)

Milgram used a volunteer sample, which is not representative of the wider population. The volunteers may have been more obedient than other participants as they had agreed to take part in the study and may have felt more obliged to continue (1 AO3 mark).
Milgram's study was reliable because it had a standardised procedure, which makes it easy to repeat and get the same results (1 AO3 mark).
The study has experimental validity, as the participants believed the shocks were real. The fact that participants showed signs of distress such as nervous laughter shows that they believed the shocks were real (1 AO3 mark).
Milgram's study lacks ecological validity as it involved an artificial situation and mundane realism as people are not normally asked to give electric shocks to another person for wrong answers on a word pair task (1 AO3 mark).

Evaluate Milgram's basic study (8 marks)

Milgram was investigating obedience (1 AO1 mark). He recruited 40 male participants via an advert in a local newspaper (1 AO1 mark). This makes it difficult to generalise as it was an all-male, volunteer sample from the USA. The volunteers may have been more obedient than other participants as they had agreed to take part in the study and may have felt more obliged to continue. Furthermore, males are not representative of how females would behave (1 AO3 mark).
Participants were asked to give electric shocks to Mr. Wallace. They thought the shocks were real when they were fake and they believed that Mr. Wallace was another participant when he was in fact a confederate of the experimenter (1 AO1 mark). Therefore, the participants were deceived, which is an ethical issue (1 AO3 mark). The participants were given verbal prods to continue throughout the experiment (1 AO1 mark). Many experienced distress during the experiment but felt compelled to continue giving the electric shocks. Therefore, participants were not protected from psychological harm, which is another ethical issue (1 AO3 mark). The experiment took place in a laboratory at Yale university and followed a standardised procedure (1 AO1 mark). The artificial situation means the study lacks ecological validity but the control over extraneous variables means the study has good internal validity (1 AO3 mark).

Note: AO1 marks are for knowledge and understanding and AO3 marks are for evaluating.

Chapter 1 - Clinical Psychology

Clinical psychology investigates explanations and treatments for mental disorders. It also studies issues related to the diagnosis. For example, it looks at validity and reliability of different diagnostic systems.

You need to be able to describe and evaluate the diagnosis of mental disorders with reference to deviance, dysfunction, distress and danger

Description:

Clinicians may diagnose someone with a mental disorder based on four dimensions: deviance, dysfunction, distress and danger.
Deviance refers to behaviour that goes against social norms. For example, if a person sits in a restaurant talking to themselves then this can be viewed as deviant behaviour.
Dysfunction refers to behaviour that stops someone living their life normally. For example, their behaviour might be interfering with their job or relationships.
Distress refers to behaviour that causes upset to an individual. It is important that clinicians understand what level of distress a person is feeling before diagnosis.
Danger refers to behaviour that causes personal harm or other people harm. For example, someone may attempt suicide or attack someone else.

Evaluation:

The deviance dimension can lead to the curtailing of people's human rights as social norms can change with time. For example, in the past homosexuality was viewed as a mental disorder and now it is not. The problem with the dysfunction dimension is that people can disagree on what is considered dysfunctional behaviour. The distress dimension takes into account how an individual is feeling. It is important that clinicians consider an individual's subjective experience of distress even if they are functioning normally. The danger dimension can be difficult in diagnosis if a person engages in risky behaviour that does not cause immediate harm. Some risky behaviours can cause personal harm such as extreme sports but these do not usually lead to a diagnosis.
A problem with interviewing patients using the four dimensions is that clinicians may subjectively interpret what their patients say. Clinicians need to use standardised tests to assess symptoms.

Note 1 : Clinical interviews are unstructured or semi-structured interviews used to find out about a person's wellbeing and personal life so that they can be diagnosed correctly.

Note 2: A clinician is a health professional who directly works with patients. This could be a doctor, psychologist or nurse. Doctors who specialise in mental health are called psychiatrists and psychologists who specialise in mental health are called clinical psychologists.

You need to be able to describe the diagnostic systems: DSM V and ICD for mental health

DSM V is a manual used to diagnose mental disorders. It groups mental disorders into 'families'. For example, anorexia nervosa, bulimia nervosa and binge-eating disorder are grouped together under eating disorders. There are three sections in the manual. Section one is an introduction, section two contains the classification of the main mental disorders and section three contains other assessment measures to help with diagnosis. In section two, details are given about specific symptoms for the disorder and how long the person needs to have them before a diagnosis is made. For example, the manual says that for an individual to be diagnosed with schizophrenia, they need to show at least two of the following symptoms: (1) delusions, (2) hallucinations, (3) disorganised speech, (4) grossly disorganised behaviour, (5) negative symptoms (e.g. diminished emotional response or avolition). In addition, one of the symptoms must be delusions, hallucinations or disorganised speech. There needs to be continuous disturbance for 6 months including at least 1 month of symptoms for a diagnosis of schizophrenia to be given.

The American Psychiatric Association (APA) has attempted to make the DSM system more reliable and valid with each new version. DSM-V takes cultural issues in diagnosis into account. For example, people from different cultures and communities may exhibit symptoms of a mental disorder in a different way. DSM-V has been designed to be more comprehensive that previous versions and aims to help doctors make a diagnosis more easily. One of the main changes is that diagnosis of Asperger's syndrome has been removed from the DSM-V and is now part of one umbrella term Autistic Spectrum Disorder (ASD).

ICD-10 covers all health disorders not just mental disorders. Section F of ICD-10 is specifically for mental disorders. Like DSM-V, it groups disorders into 'families' and outlines the symptoms for each disorder. Mental disorders are given an ICD-10 code consisting of the letter F followed by 3 or more digits. For example, F50 refers to eating disorders. F50.0 refers to anorexia nervosa and F50.2 refers to bulimia nervosa.

You need to be able to discuss reliability of diagnoses in relation to diagnostic systems

A diagnosis is reliable when one clinician gives a diagnosis and another clinician gives the same diagnosis. This is called inter-rater reliability.

If different clinicians agree on the same diagnosis for the same patient using the same diagnostic system e.g. DSM then the diagnosis has inter-rater reliability.
If a clinician tests the same patient two or more times and ends up with the same diagnosis, then the diagnosis has test-retest reliability.
Issues of reliability can occur when someone who has previously been diagnosed with a mental disorder, is then re-diagnosed later as not having it. For example, it may be disturbing for a person who has been diagnosed with schizophrenia to be told later told that they do not have it. There can also be problems if one clinician diagnoses a girl as having anorexia nervosa but another disagrees.

Brown et al. (2001) found that good inter-rater reliability for anxiety and mood disorders with DSM IV.

Rosenhan's study found that DSM III was reliable for diagnosing schizophrenia as all the pseudo-patients who said they had schizophrenic symptoms were diagnosed with schizophrenia.

Silverman et al. (2001) found that the Anxiety Disorders Interview Schedule (ADIS) on DSM IV was reliable at diagnosing anxiety disorder in children.

If different diagnostic systems such as the DSM and the ICD come up with the same diagnosis, then the diagnosis can also be considered reliable.

However, Nicholls et al. (2000) looked at inter-rater reliability for eating disorders in children using ICD 10, DSM IV and the Great Ormond Street's criteria (GOS). They found poor inter-rater reliability using ICD 10 (36% only), reasonable agreement for eating disorders in children using DSM IV (64%) but much better agreement with GOS (88%). They concluded that the GOS criteria were much better for diagnosing eating disorders in children because they were developed for use with children.

Goldstein (1988) used DSM-III to re-diagnose 199 patients with schizophrenia who had been originally diagnosed using DSM–II. She found only 169 patients were re-diagnosed with schizophrenia. This suggests some problems in reliability between DSM-II and DSM-III.

Goldstein then picked a random sample of eight patients who had been re-diagnosed as having schizophrenia using DSM-III and asked two experts to re-diagnose them as well. She found a high level of agreement in diagnosis, which suggests DSM-III is reliable.

You need to be able to discuss the validity of diagnoses in relation to diagnostic systems

A diagnosis is valid if different people who are diagnosed with schizophrenia exhibit the same symptoms as each other and respond to the same treatments. A diagnosis has face validity if the person's behaviour matches what most people believe about the mental illness. For example, most people believe that someone with bi-polar disorder can be depressed on some days but hyper on others.

Rosenhan's study showed how diagnosis using DSM III wasn't valid. The pseudo-patients did not have schizophrenia but were still diagnosed with it and all but one were given a diagnosis of schizophrenia in remission on release. In the second study, real patients who did have schizophrenia were diagnosed as normal. However, DSM has been revised many times since the Rosenhan study and its validity has been improved.

A diagnosis has etiological validity if a group of people diagnosed with a mental disorder have the same factors causing it e.g. brain scans should show that most people with schizophrenia have a reduced volume of grey matter in the brain.

A diagnosis has concurrent validity if people who are diagnosed with a mental disorder show symptoms related to their mental disorder e.g. people diagnosed with paranoid schizophrenia should exhibit signs of paranoia.

A diagnosis has predictive validity if it predicts how a person will behave in the future and how they will respond to certain treatments. e.g. if a person is diagnosed with schizophrenia and then goes on to respond well to anti-psychotic drugs, then the diagnosis has predictive validity. Lahey et al. (2006) followed children over six years and found that children diagnosed with ADHD displayed behaviour consistent with their diagnosis. Therefore, their diagnosis can be said to have good predictive validity.

If a person is diagnosed with a mental disorder such as schizophrenia but then does not show any symptoms or respond to treatments for schizophrenia, then the diagnosis lacks validity. There has been a great deal of criticism about the validity of ADHD diagnoses. Some clinicians have suggested that young children who have been diagnosed with ADHD may just be displaying normal behaviour. Issues with validity may arise, if the family or mental health staff disagree with a diagnosis.

Patients may not report their symptoms correctly because they're embarrassed or distrust the clinician. They may also not remember their symptoms correctly. This can cause problems with the validity of the diagnosis.

Clinicians may interpret symptoms differently depending on their clinical background. For example, one clinician may focus on childhood experiences and interpret anorexic behaviour as being related to family relationships whereas another clinician might focus on thoughts patterns and give a more cognitive explanation for anorexia.

You need to be able to describe the symptoms and features of schizophrenia, including thought insertion, hallucinations, delusions, disordered thinking

Features

Approximately 1% of the population suffers from schizophrenia. Goldstein found that males tend to suffer more severely from schizophrenia than females. Schizophrenia tends to onset in men between 16 to 25 years old whereas females tend to develop it about 10 years later on average. The incidence of schizophrenia in males and females is similar.

Symptoms

Schizophrenics may suffer from thought disturbances. For example, they may believe an outside force is putting thoughts into their head (thought insertion).

Another symptom of schizophrenia is hallucinations, which involves a person perceiving something that isn't real. Auditory hallucinations are the most common but people can have hallucinations through all five senses. Auditory hallucinations may involve a person hearing a voice(s) that comment on their behaviour or tell them what to do.

Delusions occur when a person has false beliefs. For example, they may have delusions of grandeur where they imagine they are prime minister or delusions of persecution where they think they are being plotted against.

Disordered thinking is when a person cannot organise their thoughts about a situation and so they behave or talk in a confused way.

Positive symptoms are diagnosed by their presence i.e. a 'normal' person does not hear voices, so hearing voices is a positive symptom. Negative symptoms are diagnosed by their absence i.e. a 'normal' person is able to show appropriate emotions so the absence of being able to show emotions is a negative symptom. Alogia (poverty of speech) and flattened effect (lack of emotional responses) are negative symptoms of schizophrenia.

Exam Tip: Do not just list symptoms of schizophrenia. Instead, explain fewer symptoms in more detail and give examples.

You need to be able to describe and evaluate the function of neurotransmitters as an explanation for schizophrenia

Description
A number of neurotransmitters have been linked to the symptoms of schizophrenia. The dopamine hypothesis says that overactivity in the dopamine neurons leads to excessive dopamine production. Excess production of the neurotransmitter dopamine in the brain is linked to schizophrenic symptoms. The over-activity of dopamine in the synapses is particularly associated with positive symptoms of schizophrenia such as hallucinations. Negative symptoms of schizophrenia such as lack of motivation may be caused by a reduction in dopamine production in the pathway connecting the midbrain to the frontal lobes (the mesocortical pathway).

Note: Neurons are nerve cells that carry messages. The tiny gaps between nerve cells are called synapses. Neurotransmitters are chemicals that transmit messages across synapses. Dopaminergic neurons have dopamine as the neurotransmitter and these may be overactive in people with schizophrenia.

Evaluation

Studies- Autopsies have found that people with schizophrenia have a higher number of dopamine receptors in their brains, which supports the theory that increased dopamine is linked with schizophrenia.
Lieberman et al. (1987) looked at the effects of amphetamines on schizophrenic patients and found that they increased positive symptoms. This supports the dopamine hypothesis as amphetamines mimic the action of dopamine in the brain. Anti-psychotic drugs that reduce the effects of dopamine by blocking dopamine receptors have been useful in treating schizophrenia. This suggests that dopamine plays a role in schizophrenic symptoms. However, not all patients respond to these drugs and more modern drugs for schizophrenia do not block dopamine receptors but still reduce the symptoms of schizophrenia. Clozapine is a newer drug for schizophrenia that works by blocking dopamine D2 receptors and serotonin

receptors with fewer side effects than the older drugs. This suggests that schizophrenic symptoms are not just due to high levels of dopamine.
Explanation- It is difficult to say whether high levels of dopamine cause schizophrenia or whether excess dopamine is a result of having the disorder. Other mental disorders such as mania are linked with high levels of dopamine as well. Furthermore, anti-psychotic drugs can cause up-regulation where the number of dopamine receptors increases in response to the receptors being blocked. This can then increase levels of dopamine in the brain.

Note: Anti-psychotic drugs that block dopamine receptors are called dopamine antagonists.

You need to be able to describe and evaluate one other biological explanation for schizophrenia, for example the genetic explanation

Description

The genetic explanation states that genes can predispose someone to develop schizophrenia. DNA studies suggest that a number of genes are associated with schizophrenia although no single gene has been identified. People who inherit a number of these high risk genes are more likely to develop schizophrenia. The genes that are associated with schizophrenia may lead to biochemical differences in the brain such as high levels of dopamine (a neurotransmitter) in the synapses, which is linked with schizophrenia. Genetic abnormalities may also lead to structural differences in the brain that cause schizophrenia. In addition, genetic abnormalities may lead to damage to neural pathways (nerve cells carrying messages) in the brain. Behaviour that is controlled by these neural pathways may then be abnormal.

Evaluation:

Exam tip-When evaluating an explanation/theory, use studies to support or contradict the explanation and then discuss limitations of the explanation. There is also one mark for listing alternative explanations/theories.

Studies- The International Schizophrenia Consortium (2008) found that schizophrenics were more likely to have DNA missing on chromosomes 1,15 and 22 than non-schizophrenics. Hong et al. (2001) found that variation in the TPH gene (the gene involved in production of the enzyme tryptophan hydroxylase) is more common in schizophrenic patients than controls. Sherrington et al. (1988) found a gene located on chromosome 5 which has been linked in a small number of extended families where they have the disorder.
Twin studies suggest that genes can predispose someone to develop schizophrenia. Gottesman's study showed a 0.48 concordance for schizophrenia in MZ twins compared to only 0.17 concordance for DZ twins. The likelihood of schizophrenia in the general population in only 0.01, so these findings suggest a genetic basis for schizophrenia. McGue (1992) found 0.40 concordance for MZ twins. In twin studies, twins share the same environment as well as genes, so the effects of genes and environment cannot be separated.
Adoption studies also suggest that there is a genetic component in schizophrenia. Heston's study showed that 10% of adoptees who had a biological mother with

schizophrenia went on to develop it themselves. However, a problem with adoption studies is that adoptees are often selectively placed into families that are similar to their biological family. Therefore, this can make it difficult to separate out the effects of genes and the environment.

Explanation-As schizophrenia has been linked with a number of different genes, it is hard to pin down a genetic cause. There is more than one type of schizophrenia so there may be more than one cause. Furthermore, if schizophrenia was entirely caused by genetics then if one MZ twin had schizophrenia, the other one would automatically develop it but this is not the case. This suggests there must be environmental factors that lead a person to develop schizophrenia as well as genetic factors.

You need to be able to describe and evaluate one non-biological explanation for schizophrenia. For example, the cognitive explanation.

Description:

A cognitive explanation for schizophrenia is that schizophrenics have difficulties with processing information and irrational beliefs. They also have problems with metarepresentation, which is the ability to recognise one's own thoughts and behaviour as being different to someone else's. For example, a schizophrenic may not be able to distinguish between their own thoughts and someone else's speech. This can lead them to believe that other people are putting thoughts in their head (thought insertion). Schizophrenics can be paranoid and think that they are being persecuted and plotted against. This can be viewed as a metarepresentation problem as they have problems interpreting other people's behaviour and intentions. Schizophrenics can also have problems with central control. This means that they cannot suppress automatic responses to stimuli. Therefore, if they intend to carry out an action or talk on a specific topic, they may be distracted by other stimuli in their environment. For example, if you ask some schizophrenics a question, they may end up talking about a stream of loosely related things because they cannot focus on the question asked. The disorganised speech produced by schizophrenics is sometimes referred to as a 'word salad'.

Evaluation:

Studies-
Daprati et al. (1997) asked schizophrenics and non-schizophrenics to make simple hand movements without them being able to see their actual hand. At the same time, they were shown an image of either their hand or a different hand on a TV-screen. They found that schizophrenics with delusions and hallucinations could not tell the difference between their own hand and someone else's hand. This supports the idea that schizophrenics have problems distinguishing between their own actions and other people's actions (a metarepresentation problem).
Frith and Done (1986) found that schizophrenic patients with negative symptoms did worse on verbal fluency tasks (such as name as many fruits as you can). This supports the idea that schizophrenics have difficulties in information processing.

Frith and Done (1989) found that schizophrenic found it much harder to work out the errors they had made in a computer game compared to non-schizophrenics. This supports the idea that schizophrenics have problems recognising their own actions. Another study that shows that people with schizophrenia have problems with information processing is Bentall et al. (1991). They got schizophrenic and non-schizophrenic participants to come up with words or read words from a list. One week later they got the participants back. They found that schizophrenic participants with hallucinations found it very difficult to remember whether they had come up with words themselves, read them or whether the words were new. Non-schizophrenic participants were much better at this, suggesting schizophrenics suffer from difficulties in information processing.

Explanation- A problem with the cognitive explanation of schizophrenia is that it does not explain the causes of schizophrenia. There are biological explanations for schizophrenia that can explain the causes. For example, genes may predispose someone to develop schizophrenia and high levels of dopamine in the brain may cause schizophrenia.

You need to be able to describe and evaluate one biological treatment for schizophrenia, for example, drug therapy.

Description

Anti-psychotic drugs are used to treat schizophrenia. They help sedate the person and reduce the intensity of hallucinations, delusions and other psychotic behaviours. Anti-psychotics are more effective when given at the onset of symptoms. Typical anti-psychotics were the first generation of the drugs aimed to treat schizophrenia. Chlorpromazine is an example of a first generation anti-psychotic drug. These drugs act by blocking the dopamine receptors (acting antagonistically on D2 receptors). The drugs fit into the dopamine receptors in the brain blocking dopamine and preventing it being picked up (remember that excess of dopamine in the brain is related to schizophrenia). However, they caused severe side effects such as neuroleptic malignant syndrome which is potentially fatal. Atypical antipsychotics are the new generation of drugs for schizophrenia. They tend to work on dopamine and serotonin receptors and they have fewer side effects. The newer anti-psychotics such as rispiridone are effective for the positive and negative symptoms of schizophrenia.

Exam tip: You can use DESERT to help you evaluate a therapy.
Directive- Is the patient reliant on the therapist for all the answers? Is there a power imbalance? If the therapist has too much power then the treatment is directive.
Effectiveness-How effective is the therapy at treating the mental disorder? What do outcome studies show?
Side effects-Are there any side effects to the therapy?
Expense-How expensive is the therapy in terms of time and money?
Reasons-Does the therapy looks at the underlying causes/reasons for the mental disorder?
Types of people-Does the therapy only work on certain types of people?

Evaluation:

Directive-Schizophrenics living in the community are often told to take drugs by their doctors but they have control over when they take it. However, schizophrenics in hospital may be pressurised to take their drugs.

Effectiveness-Anti-psychotics allow patients to live in society avoiding long term hospital care and institutionalisation and it enables them to access other therapies such as CBT which may help cure them. Anti-psychotics also reduce the intensity of symptoms. Kane (1992) found that chlorpromazine was effective with 75% of schizophrenics. Emsley (2008) found that injecting risperidone could reduce both positive and negative symptoms of schizophrenia and led to high remission rates.

Side effects-Anti-psychotics have many side effects such as tightening of muscles, constipation, weight gain and in rare cases neuroleptic malignant syndrome, which can be fatal. Many patients stop taking anti-psychotics due to the side effects. Higher and higher doses may be required as the patient develops a tolerance to the drugs.

Expense-Anti-psychotic drugs can be expensive over the long-term but in the short-term they are not as expensive as talking therapies. Atypical anti-psychotic drugs have fewer side effects but are more expensive than typical anti-psychotic drugs.

Reasons-Anti-psychotic drugs just treat the symptoms of the schizophrenia, they don't deal with any underlying issues.

Types of people-Anti-psychotic drugs do not work on all schizophrenics. Around 25% of schizophrenics do not respond to the drugs.

You need to be able to describe and evaluate one psychological treatment for schizophrenia. For example, cognitive behavioural therapy (CBT).

Description

The cognitive part of the cognitive behavioural therapy (CBT) involves questioning and changing a schizophrenic's maladaptive thoughts/distorted beliefs. For example, the therapist might question the schizophrenic's beliefs about how powerful the voices are that they hear in their head. They might also change their faulty interpretations of the world such as the belief that everyone is out to get them. The behavioural part of the therapy involves changing their behaviour, for example, getting them to ignore the voices they hear in their head or to ignore ideas that their thoughts are being put in their head by someone else. The therapist has to accept that the patient has a different perception of reality and the aim of the therapy is to help the patient manage their misperceptions.

Evaluation

Directive-Cognitive behavioural therapy is directive as the therapist tells the patient which thoughts are faulty and how they should change them.

Effectiveness-Chadwick's (2000) study found that only 8 hours of CBT combined with anti-psychotics reduced negative beliefs about how powerful the voices were. Gould et al.'s (2001) meta-analysis concluded that CBT combined with anti-psychotics reduces positive symptoms of schizophrenia. CBT can also be used to help schizophrenics that do not respond to drugs although it is usually used in combination with drugs.

Side effects-None

Expense-CBT can be expensive as it requires a trained therapist to deliver the treatment. However, CBT can be delivered over a short period of time.

Reasons-CBT does not deal with any underlying causes of schizophrenia such as childhood issues. It just deals with changing the patient's current beliefs.

Types of people-CBT is more effective on those with positive symptoms of schizophrenia as it involves getting schizophrenics to challenge their beliefs. It does not work so well on those with negative symptoms such as poverty of speech.

You need to be able to describe the features and symptoms of anorexia nervosa.

Features

Anorexia nervosa mainly affects girls and women although it has become more common amongst boys and men in recent years. The ratio of females: males with the condition is 10:1. The condition usually develops in adolescence. Prevalence of the disorder is higher in high-income industrialised countries. There are two types of anorexia nervosa: restricting type and binge-eating/purging type. People with a restricting type of anorexia restrict how much they eat and exercise excessively. People with a binge-eating/purging type of anorexia have will eat excessively and then vomit or use laxatives to purge the food.

Symptoms

Anorexia nervosa is a refusal to maintain a minimal normal body weight for age and height. Diagnosis requires bodyweight to be less than 85% of that expected. There is an intense fear of gaining weight despite being underweight. Another factor in diagnosis is amenorrhoea, the absence of menstruation for at least three consecutive menstrual cycles. 90% of sufferers are female. Sufferers have a preoccupation with thinness, dieting and exercise.

You need to be able to describe and evaluate one biological explanation of anorexia nervosa. For example, the genetic explanation of anorexia nervosa.

Description

The genetic explanation of anorexia says that genes can predispose someone to develop schizophrenia and that is why it can run in families. There is an increased risk of developing anorexia if you have a parent, sibling or twin with anorexia. Genes may lead to biochemical imbalances in the brain such as low levels of serotonin, which is associated with anorexia. Genes may also cause structural changes in the hypothalamus, which is involved in the regulation of eating. Genetic abnormalities might also lead to damage to neural pathways (nerve cells carrying messages) in the brain. Eating behaviour that is controlled by these neural pathways may then be abnormal.

Evaluation:

Studies- Kortegaard et al. (2001) found a slightly higher concordance for anorexia nervosa in MZ twins compared to DZ twins. Holland (1984) found a higher concordance rate for eating disorders in MZ twins (55%) than DZ twins.
However, MZ twins often share a more similar environment than DZ twins so it is difficult to separate out the effects of genes from environment. The fact that MZ twins do not have a 100% concordance rate for anorexia, suggests that environment plays a significant role in the development of the disorder. Twin studies are correlational so it is difficult to establish cause and effect.

Explanation-The genetic explanation for anorexia nervosa is reductionist as it does not take into account psychological, social and cultural factors.

You need to be able to describe and evaluate one non-biological explanation of anorexia nervosa. For example, social learning theory as an explanation of anorexia nervosa.

Description

Pressure from media images may contribute to the development of anorexia nervosa. Social learning theory can explain this in terms of young people paying attention to the fact that many celebrity role models are extremely thin and retaining this information. Young people have the ability to reproduce being thin if they diet excessively and will do it if they are motivated to do so. They can see that their thin role models are famous and rich and they may think that in order to be successful like their role models they have to be thin too. They may also think that being excessively thin is necessary to be accepted. This provides the motivation to diet excessively.

Evaluation:

Studies-Lai (2000) found that the rate of anorexia increased for chinese residents in Hong Kong as the culture slowly became more westernised. This supports the idea that western thin role models lead to anorexia. Crisp et al. (1976) found that dancers and fashion models were more likely to develop anorexia nervosa, which also supports SLT. Mumford et al. (1991) found that Arab and Asian women were more likely to develop eating disorders if they moved to the West. Becker et al. (2002) found that after the introduction of Western TV channels to the island of Fiji, eating disorders previously unknown on the island began to appear.

Explanation- Social learning theory does not explain why anorexia usually develops in adolescence. Anorexia nervosa may be related to fears about growing up and family issues rather than media images. Another limitation of social learning theory as an explanation of anorexia nervosa is that everyone sees pictures of slim people, but not everyone develops eating disorders.

You need to be able to describe and evaluate one biological treatment for anorexia nervosa. For example, drug therapy.

Description

Drugs do not directly help the symptoms of anorexia but they are used to treat depression and anxiety that often occur at the same time as anorexia. This helps anorexic patients to be in a better frame of mind to respond to psychological therapies. Selective serotonin reuptake inhibitors (SSRIs) and olanzapine have been used with patients with anorexia. SSRIs are a type of anti-depressant drug and they work by inhibiting the reuptake of serotonin at the presynaptic neuron. This increases the amount of serotonin in the synapse so that more serotonin can be passed to the postsynaptic neuron. This reduces any feelings of depression that might co-occur with anorexia. Olanzapine is a more modern anti-psychotic drug (atypical anti-psychotic drug), which can be used to treat anxiety as well as schizophrenia. It is believed to block serotonin and dopamine receptors in specific areas of the brain. The drug can be used to reduce any anxiety that might co-occur with anorexia.

Evaluation

Directive-Anorexic patients in a mental health institution may feel pressurised to take their drugs.
Effectiveness-The National Institute of Health and Care Excellence (NICE) recommends that drugs should not be used as the main treatment for anorexia. The majority of studies show that drugs are not effective in treating anorexia. Ferguson et al. (1999) found no significant differences between patients taking SSRIs and those not taking them. However, Jensen and Mejlhede (2000) carried out case studies on three patients taking olanzapine and found a gradual improvement in the patients' body image.
Side effects-Anorexic patients can have heart problems due to malnutrition. Therefore, clinicians need to be particularly careful when administering drugs as some drugs can cause cardiac side effects. Another side effect of SSRIs and olanzapine is that they can cause weight gain, which can be distressing for anorexic patients.
Expense-Drugs can be expensive over the long-term but in the short-term they are not as expensive as talking therapies.
Reasons-Drugs can be used to treat comorbid conditions such as depression and anxiety but they don't they don't deal with anorexic symptoms.
Types of people-Drugs may be an inappropriate treatment for anorexic patients who don't have any accompanying depression or anxiety.

You need to be able to describe and evaluate one non-biological treatment for anorexia nervosa. For example, Rational Emotive Therapy (RET).

Description

Rational emotive therapy (RET) is based on the idea that negative, irrational thoughts can lead to abnormal (maladaptive) behaviour. It aims to replace a person's irrational thoughts with more realistic ones. It works on an ABC model, where A stands for an activating event, B for the beliefs about A and C for the consequences. For example, with an anorexic, the activating event (A) might have been that they saw their friends make fun of a girl at school for being fat. The beliefs (B) about A might have been that they thought they needed to be thin in order to be accepted and liked. The consequences (C) might be that they have started dieting excessively. During therapy, an anorexic would be questioned about their beliefs so that any irrational thoughts can be identified. The therapist then tries to change the person's beliefs so that they have a more realistic view of the world. For example, they might be asked to identify people who are not thin but well-liked. They may also be set homework, where they have to practice thinking and behaving in a more rational way.

Evaluation:

Directive-RET is directive as the therapist has a lot of power over their client, they argue with them about their beliefs and tell them how to change their thinking.

Effectiveness-RET focuses on changing present irrational thoughts rather than taking into account childhood experiences so it can work quickly to change behaviour. Brandsma et al. (1978) found that RET works well on people who are perfectionist and many anorexics have such tendencies. Silverman et al. (1992) did 89 outcomes studies of RET and found that it was more effective or equal to other types of therapy for a wide range disorders.

Side effects-None

Expense-RET requires a trained professional to deliver the treatment so it can be expensive. However, it is less expensive than psychoanalysis (free association) as it can be delivered relatively quickly.

Reason-RET does not deal with the underlying causes of anorexia. It just tries to change negative, irrational thoughts. It may be better to treats anorexics with a mixture of RET and family systems therapy as it does not take into account family relationships, which may contribute to the anorexia.

Types of people-RET can be used with most anorexics.

You need to be able to discuss how cultural effects can lead to individual differences in mental health disorders

Cultural effects such as someone's gender, race, culture or religion can lead to individual differences in mental health disorders. For example, individuals from Western cultures tend to report higher rates of social anxiety disorder than individuals from Asian cultures. People with social anxiety disorder fear embarrassing themselves. Hofan and Asnaani (2010) suggest that Taijin Kyofusho (TKS), which is prevalent in Japanese and Korean cultures, is a culture-specific expression of social anxiety disorder. Individuals with TKS are concerned with displeasing or embarrassing other people rather than themselves. As a result, they avoid social situations in the same way that those diagnosed with social anxiety disorder do.

Eating disorders are more prevalent in Western cultures. Hoek et al. (2005) found that the incidence of anorexia was much lower on the island of Curacao as it is more culturally acceptable to be overweight. Becker et al. (2002) found that the girls living on the island of Fiji started developing eating disorder symptoms after the introduction of Western TV channels, suggest that Western media images influenced the girls' body image. Nasser (1986) compared Egyptian women studying in Cairo with similar Egyptian women studying in London and found that 12% of those living in London developed eating disorder symptoms, compared to 0% in Cairo. Lai (2000) found that the rate of anorexia increased for Chinese residents in Hong Kong as the culture slowly became more westernised. Mumford et al. (1991) found that Arab and Asian women were more likely to develop eating disorders if they moved to the West. These studies suggest that the Western view that being slim equates to attractiveness influences the development of eating disorders.

You need to be able to discuss how cultural effects can lead to different diagnoses of mental health disorders affecting reliability and validity.

Cultural effects can lead to different diagnoses. For example, people from different cultures may report their symptoms in a different way. Language barriers might also lead to misdiagnosis. Neighbors et al. (2003) found that African Americans are more likely to be diagnosed with schizophrenia whereas white Americans are more likely to be diagnosed with mood disorders. Such studies suggest that there is a bias in diagnosis.

Different cultures may interpret people's behaviour in different ways, for example hearing voices in Britain would be a symptom of schizophrenia but in another culture they might see it as spiritual.

There can also be problems related to mistrust of mainly white, middle class psychiatrists. Casas (1995) found that a lot of African Americans do not like to share their personal information with people of a different race so this can lead to problems with diagnosis. In fact, African Americans are less likely to seek help from mental health professionals than white Americans (Sussman, Robins and Earls, 1987). Sue and Sue (1992) found that many Asian Americans don't like to talk about their emotions and are less likely to admit they have a problem. Cinnerella and Loewethal (1999) compared cultural influences on mental disorders between white Catholics, black Christians, Muslim Pakistanis, Orthodox Jews and Indian Hindus. They found that all the groups except the white Catholics had a fear of health professionals misunderstanding them. This means that certain groups may be less likely to seek help or talk about their issues openly with a psychiatrist.

DSM-5 aims to take into account people's cultural background when making a diagnosis. It highlights how people from different cultures display symptoms of the same mental disorder differently. For example, uncontrollable crying and headaches are symptoms of panic attacks in some cultures, while difficulty breathing is the main symptom in other cultures. DSM-5 provides clinicians with detailed information about how people from different cultures think and talk about psychological problems.

You need to show an awareness of Health and Care Professions Council (HCPC) guidelines for clinical practitioners.

In order for clinicians such as clinical psychologists to practice they need to be registered with the HCPC. The HCPC checks the character of everyone who applies for registration to make sure that they are safe and effective practitioners. This involves looking at criminal convictions, cautions and character references.

The HCPC also check the health of clinicians as this might affect their ability to practise. For example, someone with a mental health issue might not be in the right state of mind to help someone else.

In addition, the HCPC set standards for education and training.

You need to be able to describe and evaluate longitudinal methods in mental health research.

Description:

Longitudinal studies involve studying the same person or group of people over a long period of time. For example, researchers working in mental health might monitor how a treatment is affecting patients' symptoms over a period of time.

Evaluation:

An advantage of longitudinal studies is that they allow researchers to follow the development and progress of a patient or group of patients over time. There are also less likely to be participant variables as the same patients are used and their progress can be tracked. However, longitudinal studies can be expensive. Furthermore, erosion of the sample (patients dropping out of the study) may cause bias. For example, if the researchers are looking at the effects of family systems therapy on anorexic children in a deprived area over time and some children leave the study to move to a more affluent area, then that can bias the results. It is also difficult to replicate a longitudinal study and establish reliability. Furthermore, new treatments are being rapidly developed in clinical psychology, which could make the findings of longitudinal research irrelevant by the time it is published.

You need to be able to describe and evaluate cross-sectional research in mental health.

Description:

Cross-sectional studies involve gathering data at one moment in time from different groups of people so that one group is compared with another group on the same characteristics, behaviour or task i.e. a cross-sectional study might compare anorexic patients of different ages at the same time.

Evaluation:

Cross-sectional designs tend to be cheaper, quicker and more practical than longitudinal designs as participants are tested at one moment in time. However, as different participants are used in the conditions, participant variables can affect results. For example, 12-year-old anorexic girls may not be comparable with the 16-year-old anorexic girls if the 12-year-old girls had more exposure to media images of thin women.

You need to be able to describe and evaluate the use of meta-analysis in mental health research.

Description:

Meta-analyses look at the findings of a number of different studies and draw conclusions. In mental health research, a meta-analysis might be carried out to look at the effectiveness of anti-psychotics versus talking therapies for schizophrenia. For example, Gould et al.'s (2001) meta-analysis concluded that CBT combined with anti-psychotics reduces positive symptoms of schizophrenia.

Evaluation:

Meta-analyses can be carried out quickly at little cost. They are useful when there is a lot of research on a specific topic such as the effectiveness of CBT and conclusions need to be drawn. However, not all studies are equally reliable and valid and some studies may be included in a meta-analysis that distort results.

You need to be able to describe and evaluate the use of primary and secondary data.

Primary data is data that is gathered first hand. For example, when an experiment, observation or questionnaire is carried out and data is collected.

Evaluation: Primary data can be tested for reliability e.g if you gather data from a laboratory experiment; you can repeat the experiment again to see whether the data can be replicated. You can then see whether the data is reliable. Primary data is also up-to-date as it is data that is collected in the present rather taken from previous research. However, primary data takes more time and money to collect.

Secondary data is data that is gathered from a secondary source e.g. data gathered from books, journals, records etc. that already exist.

Evaluation:

It takes less time and money to gather secondary data as you don't have to carry out any studies yourself, you can just look up the data in books, journals and records. Studies that are unreliable or with a bad design can be left out in the analysis. However, secondary data can be out-of-date as it involves using data from past studies and records.

You need to be able to describe and evaluate the use of case studies

Description:

A case study is an in-depth study of one person or one group of people. A number of different techniques are used to gather data. For example, the researcher may observe, interview and carry out a number of experiments on the same person. Triangulation is used to pool data together from the different types of research method and to draw conclusions. Case studies can be used in clinical psychology to study the effects of a particular therapy or to look at individuals with unique issues.

Evaluation:

Case studies are not generalisable as they are carried out on only one person or one group of people who are often unique and not representative of the wider population. It is also difficult to replicate case studies because they involve unique individuals and the interpretation of the observations and interviews is subject to bias. Therefore it is hard to establish reliability in case studies. However, triangulation is used to draw conclusions about the same concept so this improves the reliability of the findings. An advantage of case studies is that they gather rich, detailed information about the individuals using a number of different techniques, so this increases their validity. There can be ethical issues with case studies. Often they involve studying unique individuals who are more vulnerable than normal. Therefore, researchers have to be careful to protect them from psychological distress.

You need to be able to describe and evaluate an example of a case study. Lavarenne et al. (2013) Containing psychotic patients with fragile boundaries: a single group case study.

Description:

Aim-To see whether group therapy is useful for psychotic patients with fragile ego boundaries.

Procedure-They looked at a group of six individuals who suffered from schizophrenia or schizoaffective disorder who were attending a weekly support group called the 'Thursday group'. The researchers reported on one specific session, just before Christmas when the individuals were facing a break before their next meeting. They wrote down key points about the session immediately afterwards but did not record the session.

Results- The researchers reported that the individuals showed more fragile ego boundaries during this session.

Conclusion- The patients felt more vulnerable and demonstrated more fragile ego boundaries due the increased time gap between that specific session and the next meeting. Group therapy helps individuals with psychotic disorders to develop healthier ego boundaries and a tolerance to interpersonal proximity (being close to others).

Evaluation:

Generalisability-The study is not generalisable as it was only done on one small group of psychotic patients at one specific session.

Reliability-The group therapy session would be hard to replicate and get the same results. Therefore, the study is not reliable.

Application to real life-The study suggests that group therapy helps individuals with fragile ego boundaries create firmer ego boundaries.

Validity-What the patients said during the session is open to interpretation. The group leaders may also not have remembered the session accurately as the session was not recorded and they only wrote notes at the end of the session.

Ethics-There are ethical issues as the patients in the study were particularly vulnerable and may not have given fully informed consent.

Note 1: The term ego boundary refers to distinction people make between themselves and the world and the real and unreal. Some people with schizophrenia and schizoaffective disorder have fragile ego boundaries. This means that they cannot differentiate between their own perceptions and other people's and what is real and unreal.

Note 2: People with schizoaffective disorder have psychotic symptoms such as hallucinations and delusions combined with mood disturbances such as depression or bipolar disorder.

You need to be able to describe and evaluate the use of interviews in clinical psychology.

Description:

An interview involves asking patients questions verbally. For example, an interview can be used to ask schizophrenics and their families about their symptoms and experiences. It may form the basis of a case study or as a follow-up to other research methods. Structured interviews produce quantitative data. All participants are asked the same questions in the same order. They are very similar to a questionnaire except questions are read out. An unstructured interview involves an informal or in-depth conversation. Little is planned in advance (perhaps the first couple of questions) and this allows the interviewee to explain answers and introduce new issues. Unstructured interviews obtain rich, qualitative data. A semi-structured interview involves some prepared questions but also some opportunities for interviewees to expand on their answers.

Evaluation:

Unstructured interviews tend to be valid because they allow the clinician to explore issues that the patient brings up, so there will be a focus on what the patient wants to reveal. Unstructured interviews gather qualitative data as well which means that the data is detailed and in-depth. Detailed interview data can be analysed by looking for themes but this process can be subjective. The interviewers may affect the data by the way the ask questions about the patient's symptoms or background. Patients may give socially desirable answers or not wanted to admit to certain symptoms. At another time, patients may report different symptoms so there is an issue with the reliability of interviews. Certain characteristics about the interviewer such as their dress or manner can also affect replies.

You need to be able to describe and evaluate an example of an interview. Vallentine et al. (2010) Psycho-educational group for detained offender patients: understanding mental illness.

Description:

Aim-To investigate the usefulness of teaching offender patients about their mental illness via groupwork within a high security psychiatric hospital.

Note: The patients in the study are called offender patients because they had committed a criminal offence and were in Broadmoor high-security hospital.

Procedure-The sample consisted of 42 male patients at Broadmoor high security hospital. The majority of them had psychotic disorders (64% of them had paranoid schizophrenia). They had been referred to an 'Understanding Mental Illness' group as many of them lacked information about their diagnosis. A semi-structured interview was developed to see what the patients thought about the group after they had finished the sessions. Their feedback was examined using a content analysis to pick out important themes in the patients' responses.

Result- All the patients interviewed said that they would recommend the group to others. They said that the group had helped them to understand their own behaviour and that it had been valuable to listen to other people's experiences of mental illness. The information they had been given in the group made them feel more confident about coping with their symptoms in the future.

Conclusion-Psycho-educational groupwork can have a positive impact on patients. Feedback from the patients suggests that it can make them feel more confident and empowered.

Note: Psycho-educational groupwork refers to when patients attend group sessions which teach them about symptoms, treatments, causes of their mental disorder, related difficulties and coping skills.

Evaluation:

Generalisability-Only 21 of the 31 completers of the group sessions took part in the interviews. This may have led to bias in the sample.

Reliability-The use of semi-structured interviews means that it would be difficult to repeat the interviews and get the same results. The patients may answer questions differently on a different day. However, the researchers did record their interviews so that the accuracy of their data could be checked.

Application to real life-The study suggests that psycho-educational groupwork can be helpful for offender patients dealing with a psychiatric disorder.

Validity-The researchers gathered in-depth qualitative data from the patients in semi-structured interviews. This gives the study greater validity as they would have been able to understand more fully the patients' viewpoints.

Ethics-The study dealt with vulnerable people who may have felt they had to take part in the research as they were in a high-security hospital. However, some of the patients chose not to take part in the interviews, which shows that they did feel they had the right to withdraw.

You need to be able to analyse descriptive data. This means you need to be able to to work out the mean, median, mode, range and standard deviation from a set of data.

Measures of central tendency
The mean, median and mode are called measures of central tendency.

The mean

The mean is often referred to as the average of a set of numbers. You calculate the mean by adding up all the numbers and then dividing by the number of numbers.

Consider the following data set: 12, 17, 23, 27

Add the numbers together: 12+17+23+27=79
Divide 79 by 4: 79/4 =19.75

The 'Mean' (Average) is 19.75

The median

The median is the 'middle value' in a list of numbers. To find the median, your numbers have to be listed in numerical order. If you have an odd number of numbers, the median is the middle entry in the list. If you have an even number of numbers, the median is equal to the sum of the two middle numbers divided by two.

Consider the following data set: 13, 17, 21, 8

Sort the numbers into numerical order: 8, 13, 17, 21

There is not a single middle number in this data set as there is an even number of numbers.

Therefore, add the two middle numbers, 13 and 17, and divide by two:

13+17=30
30/2=15

The median is 15

The mode

The mode is the number that occurs most frequently in a set of data. If no number is repeated, then there is no mode for the set of data.

Measures of Dispersion

The range and standard deviation are measures of dispersion. They relate to how the data is spread out or 'dispersed'.

The range

The range is the difference between the largest and smallest numbers.

Consider the following data set: 11, 15, 16, 21

Subtract the smallest number from the largest number: 21-11=10

The range is 10

The standard deviation is a way of telling how far apart or how close together the data is.

Standard deviation

Why are we interested in standard deviation?

Consider the following two data sets:
Data set 1: 28, 29, 30, 31, 32   Mean = (28+29+30+31+32)/5=30
Data set 2: 10, 20, 30, 40, 50   Mean = (10+20+30+40+50)/5=30

Both data sets have a mean of 30 but the data is spread much further apart in data set 2. Therefore, data set 2 has a larger standard deviation.

Standard deviation is a measure of dispersion, which means it's useful in determining how spread out the data is. For example, if one school has students with a high mean number of UCAS points and a very small standard deviation, that means that the all the students at this school got good A-levels. If a second school has students that have an equally high mean number of UCAS points with a very high standard deviation as well, that means that the students had a much wider range of A-level grades with some getting high grades and some getting much worse grades.

Calculating standard deviation

$$s = \sqrt{\frac{\sum(x - \bar{x})^2}{n - 1}}$$

X= each value
$\bar{X}$= mean of the data set
n = the number of values
$\sum$=sum of

For example, for the data set 46, 42, 44, 45 ,43:
1) Calculate the mean: $\bar{X}$ = (46+42+44+45+43)/5=44
2) Take away the mean from each value (x - $\bar{X}$) and then square it.
3) Add up all the (x - $\bar{X}$)² values 4+4+0+1+1=10
4) Divide the sum of all the (x - $\bar{X}$)² values by n-1: 10/(5-1)=10/4=2.5
5) Square root it all for the standard deviation, s. $\sqrt{2.5}$= 1.6

Note: Using a table can help you get your calculation right.

X	$\bar{X}$	(X - $\bar{X}$)	(X - $\bar{X}$)²
46	44	2	4
42	44	-2	4
44	44	0	0
45	44	1	1
43	44	-1	1

$\bar{X}$ = 44 $\sum$ = 10

$$s = \sqrt{\frac{\sum(X - \bar{X})^2}{n - 1}} = 1.6$$

How can you interpret standard deviation?

For datasets that have a normal distribution the standard deviation can be used to determine the proportion of values that lie within a particular range of the mean value. For such distributions, 68% of values are less than one standard deviation (1SD) away from the mean value, 95% of values are less than two standard deviations (2SD) away from the mean and 99% of values are less than three standard deviations (3SD) away from the mean.
The mean of our data set was 44 and the standard deviation (SD) is 1.6. Therefore, 68% of values in the data set lie between mean-1SD (44-1.6 =42.4) and mean +1SD

(44+1.6=45.6). 99% of the values will lie between mean-3SD (44-4.8=39.2) and mean +3SD (44+4.8=48.8).
If the data set had the same mean of 44 but a larger standard deviation e.g. 2.4, it would suggest that the values were more dispersed.

You need to understand levels of data

In order to carry out an inferential statistical test, you need to know what level of data you have. There are four levels of data: nominal, ordinal, interval and ratio. Nominal data is made up of discrete categories. For example, you have two categories such as 'action toys' and 'soft toys'. Ordinal data refers to ranked data. An example of ordinal data is when athletes' are ranked as first, second and third in race. Interval data refers to data that can be measured along a scale but does not have a true zero. For example, IQ can be measured along a scale but it does not have a true zero. In contrast, ratio data is measured on a scale that has a true zero point. For example, time can be measured along a scale and does have a true zero.

You need to know about level of significance

In psychology, a significance level of $p \leq 0.05$ is chosen.

$p \leq 0.05$ means that there is an equal or less than 5% probability that the results could have occurred due to chance.

p = the probability of the results being due to chance

$\leq$ = less than or equal to

0.05 = 1 in 20 = 5%

Psychologists prefer to use the significance level: $p \leq 0.05$ to judge whether to accept a hypothesis or not. This means that there is an equal or less than 5% probability that the results are due to chance. For example, in an experiment looking at the effect of cues on memory, a researcher might find that the group that received a cue recalled more words than the group that did not receive a cue and there is a less than 5% chance that the difference between the two groups could have been due to chance (random differences between the groups).

Sometimes researchers use the significance level: $p \leq 0.1$ to judge whether to accept a hypothesis or not. This means that there is an equal or less than 10% probability that the results are due to chance. You can see that this is less conservative than $p \leq 0.05$. It is easier for the hypothesis to be accepted even though the null hypothesis might be true. This leads to a type 1 error. Type 1 errors can lead to false positive results; accepting a hypothesis even though it is incorrect. This could lead to psychologists thinking that there is a significant difference between participant's recall when they are given a cue and not given a cue when there isn't a significant difference in recall.

Sometimes researchers use the significance level: $p \leq 0.01$ to judge whether to accept a hypothesis or not. This means that there is an equal or less than 1%

probability that the results are due to chance. You can see that this is stricter than p ≤ 0.05. It is harder for the hypothesis to be accepted even though it might actually be correct. This leads to a type 2 error. Type 2 errors can lead to false negative results; rejecting a hypothesis when it is correct. This could lead to psychologists thinking that there was no difference between participants recall when given a cue compared to no cue, when there was a significant difference.

You need to be able to use the chi-square test and understand how to compare the observed and critical values to judge significance

A chi-square test is a test of difference or association. For example, a researcher might want to investigate the differences between males and females in terms of their willingness to use mental health services. The chi-square test is used when the data level is nominal, there is an independent measures design and when you are looking for a difference between two groups. There must be a minimum of 5 scores in each category, to carry out a chi-squared test.

The experimental or alternative hypothesis should state that there will be a difference between the two groups. An example of a one tailed (directional) hypothesis is: More females will be willing to use mental health services than males.

The null hypothesis should state that there is difference between the groups e.g. There will be no difference between males and females in their willingness to use mental health services.

For a chi-square test, if the observed value is greater than the critical value shown in a table, then the null hypothesis can be rejected and the result is viewed as significant. The critical value can be found in a critical values table.

The formula for the chi-squared test is:

$$\chi^2 = \sum \frac{(O-E)^2}{E}$$

O = the frequencies observed

E = the frequencies expected

$\sum$ = *the 'sum of'*

Table to show the willingness of males and females to use mental health services:

	Male	Female	Totals
No	19	10	29
Yes	6	15	21
Totals	25	25	50

First work out the degrees of freedom (df) for this contingency table:

df= (rows-1) x (columns-1)= (2-1) x (2-1) = 1 x1= 1

A table can then be used to help in the process of working out the chi-square value:

O	E	O-E	(O-E)^2	(O-E)^2/E
19	14.5	4.5	20.25	1.40
10	14.5	-4.5	20.25	1.40
6	10.5	-4.5	20.25	1.93
15	10.5	4.5	20.25	1.93

=6.65

The calculated value of chi-square is 6.65. This is called the observed value because it has been obtained from the data observed by the researcher.

Note:
O= observed frequencies. This refers to the data collected.
E=expected frequencies. This refers to what the researcher might expect to see if there is no association between gender and willingness to use mental health services. For example, if there were 29 'No' answers. You would expect half of them to be given by females and half of them to be given by males. 29/2=14.5. Therefore the expected frequency is 14.5.

In order to find out if the observed value of 6.65 is significant or not, it must be compared to the critical value. You need to find the correct critical value in a critical values table for chi-square. Make sure you look for the critical value that corresponds for df=1 and p ≤ 0.05 for a one-tailed hypothesis. This is 2.71.

As observed value of 6.65 is bigger than the critical value of 2.71, we would say that the result is significant and more females are willing to use mental health services than males.

You need to be able to use the Spearman's Rho test

For example, a researcher might want to investigate whether there is a relationship between male brain score and aggression score.

The table below shows some example data and how d^2 can be calculated by ranking the data.

Participant number	Male brain score (A)	Aggression score (B)	Rank A	Rank B	d=Rank A-Rank B	d^2
1	56	66	9	4	5	25
2	75	70	3	2	1	1
3	45	40	10	10	0	0
4	71	60	4	7	3	9
5	62	65	6	5	1	1
6	64	56	5	9	4	16
7	58	59	8	8	0	0
8	80	77	1	1	0	0
9	76	67	2	3	1	1
10	61	63	7	6	1	1

d=the difference between the ranks
d^2= the difference between the ranks squared

The formula for Spearman's rho is:

$$r_s = 1 - \frac{6\sum d^2}{n(n^2-1)}$$

Step 1: Work out the sum of d^2. Note the symbol, $\sum$, means 'sum of'.

$\sum d^2 = 25+1+9+1+16+1+1 = 54$

Step 2: We then substitute this into the main equation with the other information. Remember n=10 as there were 10 participants.
$r_s = 1 - 6 \sum d_i^2 / n(n^2-1)$
$r_s = 1 - 6 \times 54 / 10(10^2-1)$
$r_s = 1 - (324/990)$
$r_s = 1 - 0.33$
rs = 0.67

The r_s value of 0.67 indicates a strong positive relationship between the male brain score and aggression. That is, the higher you ranked for male brain score, the higher you ranked in aggression.

Note: The Spearman correlation coefficient, r_s, can take values from +1 to -1. A r_s of +1 indicates a perfect positive correlation, a r_s of zero indicates no relationship and a r_s of -1 indicates a perfect negative correlation. The closer r_s is to zero, the weaker the relationship between the co-variables.

You need to be able to compare the observed value of r_s with the critical value. To find the critical value in a critical values table, you need to look for n=10 as there were 10 participants and $p \leq 0.05$. For Spearman's rho, the observed value of r_s need to be bigger than the critical value for the result to be significant.

You need to be able to use the Wilcoxon Signed Rank test

You use a Wilcoxon Signed Rank test when you have a repeated measures design, ordinal data and you are investigating whether there is a significant difference between two conditions. For example, a researcher wants to see whether there is a differences between two treatments for anorexics. In order to do this, they ask seven anorexic patients who have been receiving two different treatments to rate them out of 10.

Table to show rankings for therapy A and therapy B given by the same patients:

Patient	Therapy A	Therapy B
1	7	4
2	9	3
3	8	4
4	7	7
5	8	3
6	5	6
7	9	5

Step 1: Calculate the differences between two scores by taking one from the other. Then rank the differences giving the smallest difference Rank 1.

Patient	Therapy A	Therapy B	Difference between ranks (d)	Ranked differences
1	4	7	-3	2
2	9	3	6	6
3	8	4	4	3.5
4	7	7	0	ignore
5	8	3	5	5
6	5	6	-1	1
7	9	5	4	3.5

Note that the lowest rank is given to the smallest difference score (-1), ignoring whether it is a positive or negative difference.

If two or more difference scores are the same, then these scores get the average of the ranks that those scores would have obtained, had they been different from each other. Here there are two difference scores of 4. Therefore we work out the mean rank that these scores *would* have had, if they had been different from each other (the ranks of 3 and 4). The mean rank is (3+4)/2=3.5 so this is the rank that the two difference scores of 4 are given.

You do not rank any differences of 0 and when adding the number of scores, do not count those with a difference of 0.

Step 2: Add up the ranks for positive differences.

6+3.5+5+3.5=18

Step 3: Add up the ranks for negative difference.

1+2=3

Step 4: Whatever is the smallest value from step 2 and 3 is the value of T. This is your observed value.

Here T=3

Step 5: N is the number of differences, ignoring 0 differences.

There are 6 differences here.

Step 6: Look at the table of critical values for a Wilcoxon Signed Rank test. With an N of 6 for a two-tailed test at 0.05 significance, the critical value is 0.

For a Wilcoxon Signed Rank test, T has to be less than or equal to the critical value for the result to be significant. In this example, T=3 so the observed value is bigger than the critical value and the result is not significant. The null hypothesis must be accepted and so there was no significant difference between therapy A and therapy B for anorexic patients.

Note: When you are looking up critical values in a table, you need to know: whether the hypothesis was one-tailed or two-tailed; the number of participants who had a difference between their scores (shown as 'N' on the table) and the significance level. The values in the Wilcoxon Signed Rank test are termed 'T' and unlike the Spearman-rank and Chi-squared Tests the observed value has to be equal to or less than the critical value for the results to be significant (i.e. to accept the experimental hypothesis and reject the null hypothesis).

You need to be able to use the Mann-Whitney test

You use a Mann-Whitney U test when you have an independent groups design, ordinal data and you are testing for a difference between two groups.

Mann-Whitney U test formulae

$$U_a = n_a n_b + \frac{n_a(n_a+1)}{2} - \sum R_a$$

$$U_b = n_a n_b + \frac{n_b(n_b+1)}{2} - \sum R_b$$

(U is the smaller of U_a and U_b)

n_a is the number of participants rating in group A
n_b is the number of participants in group B
$\sum R_a$ is the sum of the ranks for group A's data
$\sum Rb$ is the sum of the ranks for group B's data

For example, a researcher might ask two groups of schizophrenic patients receiving different therapies to rate their treatment out of 10. There are two conditions, with each participant taking part in only one of the conditions so it is an independent groups design. The data are ratings (ordinal data) and so the Mann-Whitney U test is appropriate.

Table to show rankings for therapy A versus therapy B:

Participants	Therapy A	Participant	Therapy B
1	3	1	9
2	4	2	7
3	2	3	5
4	6	4	10
5	2	5	6
6	5	6	8

Step 1: Rank all the scores together.

Note: For a Mann-Whitney U test, the data from both groups are ranked together. If participants have the same score, they are given the same rank. This way of ranking is different to how data is ranked for the Spearman's rho test.

Participant	Therapy A Rating	Rank	Participant	Therapy B Rating	Rank
1	3	3	1	9	11
2	4	4	2	7	9
3	2	1.5	3	5	5.5
4	6	7.5	4	10	12
5	2	1.5	5	6	7.5
6	5	5.5	6	8	10

Step 2: Calculate Ua by first adding up all the ranks for therapy A to calculate $\sum R_a$:

$\sum R_a = 3 + 4 + 1.5 + 7.5 + 1.5 + 5.5 = 23$

Step 3: Multiply the number of participants in group A (n_a) by the number of participants in group B (n_b)

Note: $n_a n_b$ means n_a multiplied by n_b

$n_a \times n_b = 6 \times 6 = 36$

Step 4: Calculate $n_a (n_a+1)$

$n_a+1 = 6+1 = 7$
Multiply n_a+1 by n_a
As $n_a+1 = 7$ and $n_a = 6$
$n_a (n_a+1) = 7 \times 6 = 42$

Step 5: Calculate $n_a (n_a+1)/2$
Divide $n_a (n_a+1)$ by 2
$42/2 = 21$

Step 6: Calculate $U_a = n_a n_b + n_a (n_a+1)/2 - \sum R_a$

$n_a n_b = 6$
$n_a (n_a+1)/2 = 21$
$\sum R_a = 23$

So $U_a = 21+36-23 = 34$

Step 7: Calculate Ub by first adding up the the ranks for therapy B to calculate $\sum R_b$:

$\sum R_b = 11 + 9 + 5.5 + 12 + 7.5 + 10 = 55$

Step 8: You already know that $n_a n_b = 36$ from step 3
You already know $n_b(n_b+1)/2 = 21$ from step 5 as there are the same number of participants in group B as in group A.
You know from step 7 that $\sum R_b = 55$
So $U_b = n_a n_b + n_b(n_b+1)/2 - \sum R_b = 36+21-55 = 2$

Step 9: U is the smaller of U_a and U_b.
So as U_b is the smallest value, U_b is the value of U.
Therefore, U=2

Step 10: Look up the critical values in a critical values table for $n_a=6$ and $n_b=6$. This is the number of participants in each group.

To be significant, U has to be equal to or less than the critical value. The critical value for a two tailed test at 0.05 significance level = 5 and the critical value for a two tailed test at 0.01 significance level = 2 So, U is less than the critical value of U for a 0.05 significance level. It is also equal to the critical value of U for a 0.01 significance level.

This means that there is a highly significant difference between therapy A and therapy B.

Note: When you are looking up critical values in a table, you need to know: whether the hypothesis was one-tailed or two-tailed; the number of participants in each condition (shown as 'N' on the table) and the significance level. The values in the Mann-Whitney Test are termed 'U' and unlike the Spearman-rank and Chi-squared Tests the observed value has to be equal to or less than the critical value for the results to be significant (i.e. to accept the experimental hypothesis and reject the null hypothesis).

You need to be able to analyse qualitative data using thematic analysis.

A thematic analysis can be used to analyse different types of data, from media articles to transcripts of focus groups or interviews. It is suitable for analysing people's experiences, opinions and perceptions. It can also be used to look at how different issues and concepts are constructed or represented. The types of research questions in clinical psychology that might lead to a thematic analysis of the data are: 'How is mental illness portrayed in the media?' and 'What are women's experiences of dealing with depression?'
There are a number of stages in carrying out a thematic analysis: 1) The researcher familiarises themselves with the data by reading it several times; 2) Codes are generated for important features of the data; 3) The researcher looks for themes by examining the codes and collated data to identify broader patterns of meaning (potential themes); 4) The themes are reviewed by checking them against what

people have said. At this stage, themes may be refined or discarded; 5) Themes are named and a detailed analysis of each theme is carried out; 6) Finally, the themes are written up with quotes from the data collected. The analysis is linked to existing theories.

Evaluation:

A thematic analysis can be used for a wide range of research questions. Rich, detailed data can be obtained, which can lead to a deeper insight into people's experiences, opinions and representations. However, thematic analyses are open to interpretation and hence subjective. They can be hard to replicate and so they have problems with reliability.

You need to be able to analyse qualitative data using grounded theory.

Grounded theory uses an inductive method to develop theories. This is different to the scientific method of generating hypotheses first and testing them. Grounded theory involves the researcher collecting data from a specific area of interest and over time advancing theories. For example, a researcher might investigate how families respond to mental illness by interviewing them. They will then look for codes and categories that emerge from the data. Finally, the researcher might suggest some ideas about how families respond to mental illness.

When analysing qualitative data, the researcher initially assigns codes to every unit of information, for example, each sentence, argument or observation. For example, when Rose et al. (2002) looked at how families responded to mental illness, one family member said, 'We can't and shouldn't do it all.' This could be given the code of 'accepting limitations'. The codes should be specific and not too broad.

Once the researcher has decided which codes are most important or prevalent, they will apply these codes to other data from interviews, articles and observation. This is called focused coding and the aim is to refine, modify and understand the codes in more detail.

The next stage is to identify categories. For example, codes such as 'accepting limitations' and 'inability of the person with the mental illness to look after themselves' might be related to the broader category of 'resolving questions of responsibility'.
The researcher will also write memos as they go along, which are their personal ideas and thoughts that emerge as they reflect on the coding process. This helps the researcher to clarify their ideas. Memos about codes and categories are integrated and refined.
Eventually, the researcher will develop their own theories. For example, Rose et al. (2002) concluded from their research that the families pursued normalcy. This means that the families of people with mental disorder engage in an effort to help the patient be normal.

Evaluation:

Grounded theory has been criticised for being unscientific and subjective. Researchers may interpret the evidence in a biased way especially if they are trying to fit the data with their emerging theories. Another researcher might interpret the evidence in a different way and so the research can lack reliability. A further issue with grounded theory as a method is that it can take a long time to gather and analyse the information. However, if the theory is 'grounded' in evidence then it should have good validity.

You need to be able to describe and evaluate the classic study: Rosenhan (1973) On being sane in insane places

Description:

Aim: To see whether the sane can be distinguished from the insane using the DSM classification system. Rosenhan wanted to see whether clinicians would be able to tell the difference between a patient suffering from a real mental disorder and a healthy 'pseudopatient.'

Procedure: Rosenhan and seven volunteers arrived at a range of hospitals reporting a single symptom, hearing voices saying 'empty', 'hollow' and 'thud.' They gave real information about themselves such as details about their families and childhood. However, they gave false names and those in the medical profession gave a false occupation. As soon as the eight pseudopatients were in hospital, they started behaving normally.

Results: All the pseudopatients were admitted and none were detected as being sane. It was an average of 19 days before any of them were released. Even when they were released all but one were given the diagnosis of schizophrenia in remission. In no case did any of the doctors and nurses notice that there was nothing wrong with them.

Conclusion: Rosenhan concluded that staff in psychiatric hospitals were unable to distinguish those who were sane from those who were insane and that DSM is not a valid measurement of mental illness.

Evaluation:

Generalisability-The study was carried out in 1973 so the findings of the study may not apply to the present day. The DSM had been revised many times since 1973 to improve its validity. Furthermore, doctor-patient relationships have changed.
The pseudo-patients had insisted on being admitted to the hospital themselves so the psychiatrists may have been more cautious about releasing them. Not all people diagnosed with schizophrenia ask to be admitted to a hospital so the treatment of the pseudo-patients may not be representative of how other patients would be treated. The psychiatrists would have also been careful about releasing an individual who had only recently been admitted too fast. However, a wide range of hospitals were used so the results can be generalised to other psychiatric hospitals at the time.

Reliability-The study was conducted in the field so extraneous variables were hard to control and so the study would be difficult to repeat.

Application to real life-The study highlighted problems with DSM and how psychiatric patients are treated in hospital.

Ecological validity-The study had ecological validity as it was carried out the doctors' and nurses' normal working environment (psychiatric hospitals) so they would have behaved naturally.

Experimental validity-The doctors and nurses in the psychiatric hospital were unaware the patients were fake so they would not have displayed any demand characteristics. Therefore, the study has good experimental validity. However, the fact that the pseudopatients were released with the diagnosis of 'schizophrenia in remission' shows that the psychiatrists did recognise something different about them as this is a rare diagnosis for real patients.

Ethics-There are a number of ethical issues with the study. The hospital staff were deceived about the pseudopatients' symptoms and they did not know they were in a study so they were unable to give consent. However, Rosenhan did protect the anonymity of the staff and hospitals afterwards.

You need to be able to describe and evaluate one contemporary study on schizophrenia. Carlsson et al. (1999) Network interactions in schizophrenia – therapeutic implications.

Description:

Aim-To review research on the effects of the neurotransmitters dopamine and glutamate on the symptoms of schizophrenia.

Procedure-The researchers looked at a number of different studies to assess whether high levels of dopamine (hyperdopaminergia) and/or low levels of glutamate (hypoglutamatergia) are linked to schizophrenia.

Results-There is evidence to support the hyperdopaminergia and hypoglutamatergia models of schizophrenia. Clozapine which blocks the activity of dopamine and serotonin has been found to be a more effective treatment for schizophrenia than drugs that block the activity of dopamine alone. This may be because levels of serotonin have an affect on levels of glutamate.

Conclusion: As neurotransmitters such as glutamate and serotonin are linked to the symptoms of schizophrenia, developing drugs that work on these neurotransmitters as well as dopamine is important. Newer drugs may be able to avoid the side effects related to anti-psychotic drugs that work on dopamine alone.

Evaluation:

Generalisability-The review looked at a number of different studies. The use of many studies makes the findings more generalisable to the wider population.

Reliability- Not all studies used in the review may have been equally reliable. However, the studies used in the review were scientific such as PET scans and this makes the review more reliable.

Application to real life-The review suggests that new drugs that act on different neurotransmitters should be developed for schizophrenia.

Validity-Not all the studies used in the review may have been equally valid, which could distort the overall findings. However, using evidence from a large number of studies can give more valid conclusions about the effect of different neurotransmitters on the symptoms of schizophrenia.

Ethics-As secondary data was used, there are no ethical issues with this study.

You need to be able to describe and evaluate one contemporary study on anorexia. For example, Guardia et al. (2012) Imagining One's Own and Someone Else's Body Actions: Dissociation in Anorexia Nervosa.

Description:

Background: Previous research has shown that patients with anorexia nervosa overestimate their own body size.

Aim- To see whether anorexic patients make incorrect judgements about their own body only or whether they also had a distorted perception of other people's bodies too.

Procedure-50 young female participants were used: 25 anorexic participants and 25 control participants. The two groups were matched for age and educational level. 51 different door-like apertures (varying from 30 cm to 80 cm in width) were projected onto a wall so that it looked like a realistic 2m high doorway.
The participants had to judge whether or not the doorway was wide enough for them to pass through (i.e. first-person perspective) without turning sideways. They then had to judge whether the doorway was big enough for another person present in the testing room to pass through (i.e. third-person perspective).

Results-Anorexic patients showed a distorted view of their own body size and would frequently say that they couldn't fit through a doorway that was considerably bigger than them. However, when the anorexic patients were asked to judge whether another person could go through a doorway, they were more accurate. The control group showed no significant difference when judging whether they or someone else could pass through a doorway.

Conclusion- Anorexic patients overestimate their own body size but not other people's. The researchers suggest that anorexic patients' perception of their body size does not change even when they have lost weight because their brain has not updated their body size quickly enough.

Evaluation:

Generalisability-The sample was small so it is hard to generalise to all anorexic patients. The participants were all young females so the findings can't be generalised to male anorexic patients or older anorexic patients. However, most anorexic patients are young females so the using a young female sample is representative of the majority of anorexic patients.

Reliability-The study followed a standardised procedure which makes it easy to replicate and test for reliability.

Application to real life-The study suggests that therapists should help change anorexic patients' perceptions and thoughts about their body size.

Validity-In the third-person perspective condition, when participants had to estimate another person's ability to pass through the doorway, the control group were closer in size to the other person than the anorexic patients. This may have been why the anorexic patients made more errors about the other person's ability to pass through the doorway.

Ethics-Some of the participants were under 18 and were particularly vulnerable. It would have been important to make sure the results were discussed in a sensitive way.

You need to be able to describe one key question of relevance to today's society, discussed as a contemporary issue for society rather than an academic argument and apply concepts, theories and research to it. For example, 'How are mental health issues portrayed in the media?'

The media has a powerful influence on how people perceive mental health issues. If television programmes, films, magazines and newspapers portray those with mental health problems in a negative way then this can have an impact on whether people with mental health issues seek help and how people respond to those with mental health problem.
Philo et al. (1994) analysed media coverage of mental health issues and found that it perpetuated negative stereotypes of people with mental disorders. Pirkis and Francis (2012) looked at how newspapers reported mental illness in Australia and found that the most common theme related to 'disorder, crisis and risk'. Dietrich et al. (2006) found that students who read a negative article about mental illness felt more negative attitudes toward people with mental illness. They also found that those students who watched more TV were more wary of those with mental health issues. Wahl et al. (2007) found that many children's TV programmes depicted characters with mental illness as aggressive and threatening.
Rosenhan's study found that when the pseudopatients were admitted to hospital and began to behave normally, it was difficult for them to escape the label they had been given. They were released with the diagnosis of schizophrenia in remission rather than not having schizophrenia at all and their normal behaviour was interpreted as being related to schizophrenia. People with mental health issues may be worried about being labelled especially if there are negative stereotypes in the media.

On the other hand, there has been some positive media coverage of mental health issues. Some celebrities such as Stephen Fry have talked about their mental health issues publicly. This helps to reduce the stigma about having a mental health problem and combats negative stereotypes.

'Time to change' is a mental health campaign that aims to raise awareness and understanding of mental health issues. Surveys have shown that the 'Time to Change' campaign has improved attitudes towards people with mental illness. In 2013, 64% of people acknowledged that they knew someone with a mental health problem compared to 58% in 2009.

You need to be able to describe one practical research exercise to gather data relevant to topics covered in clinical psychology. This practical research exercise must adhere to ethical principles in both content and intention. Example practical: A content analysis that explores attitudes to mental health

Aim: To investigate how mental illness is portrayed in the media. To undertake a content analysis of two newspaper articles discussing mental health issues.

How was the data gathered and analysed?

The content analysis involved looking for articles on the internet about mental illness. The phrases 'mental health issues and 'mental illness' were put into the google search bar. The articles were chosen because they were from newspapers with different political and ideological agendas. The Guardian is a left-wing newspaper and The Daily Telegraph is a right-wing newspaper.

How was the data analysed?

Positive and negative comments in each article were tallied and mean number of positive and negative comments calculated for each article. The articles were then compared in terms of mean number of positive and negative comments to see whether there was any agreement between the articles.

Results: The Telegraph had fewer positive comments and more negative comments about mental health.

	Mean no. of positive comments	Mean no. of negative comments
The Guardian	3.3	2.4
The Telegraph	2.1	3.1

Conclusion: Both articles had negative stereotypes about mental illness. The political ideology of the media articles was reflected in how positive or negative they were about mental health issues.

You need to be able to discuss ethical issues in clinical psychology

There are ethical issues with working with people with mental health issues as they are more vulnerable. It is particularly important that they are not caused any psychological distress. As part of a clinical trial assessing the effectiveness of a treatment, some patients may be put in a control group who receive a placebo treatment or a less effective treatment. From an ethical standpoint, these patients should be given the best possible treatment as soon as the trial has ended.

You need to be able to discuss practical issues in the design and implementation of research

Qualitative data collected from interviews, observations or case studies of patients is less reliable than quantitative data. However, such data is more valid as it takes into account the patient's opinion and experiences about their illness or treatment.

You need to be able to discuss reductionism

Many treatments in clinical psychology are reductionist because they focus on only one cause of mental disorder. For example, drug therapy is reductionist because it only looks at biological factors in mental disorder not social or psychological. Cognitive behavioural therapy is reductionist because it sees the causes of mental disorder as being related to to irrational beliefs and does not take into account biological or social factors.

You need to be able to compare different factors/themes used to explain mental disorder

There are many different explanations of schizophrenia. One biological factor that can lead someone to develop schizophrenia is high levels of the chemical dopamine in the brain. However, there is evidence that cognitive factors are involved in schizophrenia too. For example, people with schizophrenia have problems with processing information. In contrast, a psychodynamic perspective would argue that poor communication in families causes schizophrenia.

You need to be able to discuss clinical psychology as a science

Biological treatments such as drug therapy are considered more scientific than talking therapies such as family systems therapy. Biological explanations of mental disorder such as the dopamine hypothesis for schizophrenia are more scientific than psychodynamic explanations as they are based on scientific evidence such as brain scans.

You need to be able to discuss cultural issues in clinical psychology

Cultural issues such as country of origin, race, gender and religion can affect the way people report mental health symptoms. These cultural effects can lead to different diagnoses. DSM V takes into account cultural issues in diagnosis.

You need to be able to discuss the nature-nurture debate in clinical psychology

Nature refers to how our genes and biology affect our development. For example, the extent to which mental illness is related to our genes, brain structure and neurotransmitters.

Nurture refers to how our environment affects our development. For example, the extent to which mental illness is based on our family environment and experiences.

The stress-diathesis model suggests that genes may predispose us to mental illness but we also need stressors in our environment in order to trigger the illness. Most psychologists agree that both biological and environmental factors are involved in the development of mental health issues.

You need to be able to understand how psychological knowledge has developed over time in clinical psychology

Each version of DSM has tightened up the criteria for diagnosis and included more mental disorders. DSM V has taken into account cultural issues in diagnosis. One of the main changes is that diagnosis of Asperger's syndrome has been removed from the DSM-5 and is now part of one umbrella term Autistic Spectrum Disorder (ASD). This is to recognise that those previously diagnosed with Asperger's syndrome and autism showed similar traits. Treatments also change over time. For example, newer drugs for schizophrenia have fewer side effects.

You need to be able to discuss issues of social control in clinical psychology

Treatments can be used to control people so that they conform to society's norms. For example, when drugs such as Ritalin are used to treat children with ADHD, this could be regarded as social control as the drugs are used to 'normalise' their behaviour. Some argue that as increasing numbers of younger and younger children are being diagnosed with ADHD, it is not a problem with the children but with society.

You need to be able to discuss the use of psychological knowledge in society

Research in clinical psychology has led to the development of many treatments. Drug therapy combined with talking therapies enable people with mental health issues to live in the community without being institutionalised. Understanding the causes of mental disorder has also contributed to wider acceptance of those who suffer from mental health problems.

You need to be able to discuss socially sensitive research

Sieber and Stanley define socially sensitive research as: 'Studies in which there are potential consequences or implications, either directly for the participants in the research or for the class of individuals represented by the research'. Research looking at the incidence of particular mental disorders in certain races, cultures or genders could be classed as socially sensitive research as it could lead to labelling of certain groups in society.

Student answer to exemplar exam question in Clinical Psychology:

Describe one treatment for schizophrenia from the Biological Approach. Evaluate this treatment using research evidence. (12 marks)

Note: The question asks for one treatment only and how it can be used to treat one mental disorder only.

Student answer:

Drug therapy can be used by the psychiatrist to treat schizophrenia. Anti-psychotic drugs are used with schizophrenics to block the effects of dopamine. The neurotransmitter dopamine is involved in cognitive functions such as attention and problem-solving. Dopamine in the frontal lobes of the brain, controls the flow of information from other areas of the brain. Therefore, by reducing the availability of dopamine in the brain, anti-psychotic drugs can reduce symptoms related to information processing such as thought disorders. It is thought that both typical and atypical anti-psychotics work by inhibiting dopamine at the receptor level. Typical anti-psychotics such as chlorpromazine could reduce the symptoms of schizophrenia but cause severe side effects. Atypical antipsychotics (newer drugs) reduce the symptoms of schizophrenia but with fewer side effects. Clozapine is an example of a new generation anti-psychotic drug.

Anti-psychotic drugs can help schizophrenics to manage their symptoms and to live in the community. They tend to act quickly and can stabilise a patient so that they can access other treatments such as cognitive behavioural therapy. However, a problem with anti-psychotic drugs is that they can have unpleasant side effects, which can cause schizophrenics to stop taking the drugs. Patients can develop a tolerance to the drugs so that they need higher doses for the drugs to work. There is also the criticism that anti-psychotics only sedate patients rather than really cure them. Atypical anti-psychotic drugs have fewer side effects but are more expensive than typical anti-psychotic drugs. Anti-psychotic drugs do not work on all schizophrenics.
Level 4 answer: 10 out of 12 marks

Commentary:

This student describes how anti-psychotics can be used to treat schizophrenia well. However, there could also have been some discussion of practical considerations. For example, they could have discussed how psychiatrists prescribing anti-psychotic drugs need to carefully monitor how a patient is responding to them. The psychiatrist may then need to adjust the dosage or even try out a different type of anti-psychotic.

This student could also have used some studies to support their evaluation. Kane (1992) found that chlorpromazine was effective with 75% of schizophrenics. Emsley (2008) found that injecting risperidone could reduce both positive and negative symptoms of schizophrenia and led to high remission rates. The effectiveness of atypical anti-psychotics for schizophrenia in terms of number of re-hospitalisations is similar to that of typical anti-psychotics. Stargardt et al. (2008) found that atypical anti-psychotics were only cost-effective in severe cases as it was only in these cases that the atypical anti-psychotics reduced re-hospitalisations.

Chapter 2-Criminological Psychology

Criminological psychology investigates explanations and treatments for criminal and anti-social behaviour. It also looks at issues related to the justice system and the way criminals are convicted including problems with eyewitness testimony and how jury and defendant characteristics affect sentencing.

A Crime: is when someone commits an act against the law, for example, stealing a car.

Anti-social behaviour: refers to behaviour that causes problems for other people but is not necessarily against the law. An example of anti-social behaviour is when teenagers gather together outside a shop and behave in a rude way to passing customers.

Recidivism: is when a person commits a crime they have already been punished for. An example of recidivism is when a criminal goes to prison for stealing and then steals again on release.

Stereotyping: is judging an individual based on their membership of group when there is limited experience of the group. Based on these stereotypes people are **labelled**. For example, a boy in a hoodie may be labelled as a troublemaker based on his appearance.

You need to be able to describe and evaluate brain injury as a biological explanation of criminal behaviour

Description:

A brain injury caused by an accident, illness or long-term substance misuse may lead to criminal or aggressive behaviour. Brain injury can lead to changes in personality dependent on the area of the brain that has been damaged. For example, Phineas Gage, a railway worker became much more aggressive after his frontal lobe was damaged in a railway accident.

Evaluation:

Studies-Williams et al. (2010) investigated the incidence of brain injury amongst prisoners and found that 60% of them had suffered some kind of brain injury. This suggests that having a brain injury can affect aggression levels, impulse control and judgement, leading to a higher likelihood of engaging in criminal behaviour. Explanation-It is difficult to establish a cause and effect relationship between brain injury and criminal or aggressive behaviour as there may be other factors involved. For example, those who have a brain injury due to alcohol or drug abuse may be more likely to engage in criminal or aggressive behaviour due to the substance misuse rather than the brain injury. Furthermore, people who engage in substance misuse may have other issues that affect their behaviour such as poor family relationships or personality disorders.

You need to be able to describe and evaluate the amygdala as a biological explanation of aggressive behaviour

Description:

The amygdala is a part of the brain involved in regulating emotions. Therefore, damage to this part of the brain can lead to problems with how people express emotion. For example, they may behave in an overly emotional way or show a lack of emotion. Having a smaller amygdala is linked with a lack of empathy for others and aggression. Research shows that psychopaths tend to have smaller amygdalae.

Evaluation:

Studies-Bard (1940) lesioned the brains of cats and found that the hypothalamus and amygdala were responsible for aggression. However, there are problems with generalising animal research to humans as humans are more complex. For example, the prefrontal cortex in animals is smaller than in humans.

Swantje et al. (2012) found that women with smaller amygdalas were more likely to have higher aggression scores. This supports the idea that the amygdala plays an important role in aggression.
Raine et al. compared the brains of murderers and non-murderers and found that differences in the functioning of the amygdala.

Explanation-Having a smaller amygdala does not mean that you will necessarily engage in criminal or aggressive acts. Humans have the ability to control their behaviour and environmental influences affect behaviour too.

You need to be able to describe and evaluate XYY syndrome as a biological explanation of criminal and anti-social behaviour

Description:

Males have the sex chromosomes XY and are more governed by androgens (such as testosterone). Females have the sex chromosomes XX and are more governed by oestrogens. XYY syndrome is when some males are born with an extra Y chromosome. About 1 in 1000 males will have an extra Y chromosome. It has been suggested that males with XYY genes have lower IQs and are more aggressive.

Evaluation:

Studies-Thielgaard (1984) found that men with XYY chromosomes had lower IQs. She suggested that it was these men's learning difficulties that made them more likely to engage in criminal or anti-social behaviour. The study also showed that only a small proportion of criminals had the XYY syndrome.
Explanation-As most of the prison population is made up of men and women without XYY chromosomes, the syndrome cannot explain criminal behaviour in these groups.

You need to be able to describe and evaluate labelling and the self-fulfilling prophecy as a social explanation of criminal and anti-social behaviour

Description:

The self-fulfilling prophecy (SFP) is a prediction that comes true because it has been made. For example, when people become what others expect them to become. The self-fulfilling prophecy explains criminal or anti-social behaviour as arising due to other people's expectations. A person may be labelled as a criminal or a troublemaker due to stereotypes and they may be treated differently as a result. The person may find it difficult to escape this label and so they internalise it and it becomes part of their self-concept. Once a criminal or anti-social label becomes part of the person's self-concept, they may behave according to the label and carry out criminal or anti-social acts. For example, a young person dressed in a hooded top may be stereotyped as anti-social. People may be more wary of them and avoid them in the street. The antisocial label may then become part of their identity and they may actually go on to behave in an anti-social way.

Evaluation:

Studies-Jahoda's (1954) study supports the self-fulfilling prophecy. The Ashanti tribe of West Africa believe that boys born on a Wednesday are more aggressive and boys born on a Monday are calm. Jahoda (1954) examined police records and found that males born on Wednesday had higher arrest rates than those born on Monday suggesting that the tribe's expectations did affect their behaviour. Madon (2004) questioned parents about how much alcohol they expected their children to drink in the next year and found that if parents expected their children to drink too much alcohol, they did. This study can be viewed as support for the self-fulfilling prophecy. However, it may be that parents who drink a lot themselves expect their children to drink more too. Their children may just be copying their behaviour rather than there being a self-fulfilling prophecy. Madon and Jahoda's studies are correlational and therefore cannot establish a causal link between expectations and later behaviour. Rosenthal and Jacobsen (1968) carried out an experiment which supports the self-fulfilling prophecy. They found that when teachers believed certain children in their class were more intelligent, their IQ scores rose. A similar process may occur if children are labelled as naughty or troublemakers.

Explanation-A limitation of the self-fulfilling prophecy is that people with a strong self-image are unlikely to be affected by other people's negative expectations. There are many other reasons for criminal and anti-social behaviour that the self-fulfilling prophecy does not take into account such as observing criminal or anti-social role models (social learning theory), genes, high levels of testosterone, poverty, status and culture.

You need to be able to describe and evaluate the cognitive interview

Description:

If police officers use leading questions during interviews with witnesses, this can lead to inaccuracies later. Therefore, the cognitive interview has been developed to improve witnesses' recall of events. During a cognitive interview, witnesses are asked to freely recall as much information as they can remember and to describe everything they could see, hear, smell or touch. Witnesses are also asked to recall events in different orders and from different perspectives. Open ended questions are used rather than leading ones e.g. What happened next? The cognitive interview is based on Tulving's encoding specificity principle, which suggests that recall is better if a person has the same cues at retrieval as they had when they encoded the information. By getting witnesses, to mentally reinstate the context of an incident using cues such as sight, sound, smell and touch, they should be able to recall the incident better.

Evaluation:

Stein and Memon (2006) and Geiselman (1986) found that the cognitive interviews increases both the quality and quantity of information recalled by witnesses. Research has also shown that people questioned using cognitive interviews are less likely to be influenced by leading questions.
On the other hand, Milne (1997) found that the cognitive interview did not lead to better recall than normal interviewing techniques.
However, the effectiveness of cognitive interviews may be affected by the fact that police officers do not always use all the elements of the cognitive interview properly as it is very time-consuming.

You need to be able to describe ethical interview techniques

In the past, the police used psychological manipulation in order to gain confessions or supporting evidence for a conviction. As a result, some innocent people were convicted of crimes they did not commit. Nowadays, the police are advised to use interview practices which improve the truthfulness of the information given. For example, the police are trained to avoid asking witnesses leading questions and to use techniques which improve memory.

You need to be able to describe and evaluate the use of psychological formulation to understand the function of offending behaviour in the individual

Psychologists may be asked to come up with a psychological formulation for a why an offender committed a crime. The psychological formulation may consist of biological reasons, social circumstances, relationships and life events that might have led to the person committing the crime. Formulations usually take into account different psychological theories for explaining behaviour. For example, an individual may get into a fight in pub and end up killing another person. A psychological formulation might take into account the individual's high testosterone levels, the breakdown of a romantic relationship and their family history of domestic violence.

Evaluation:

It is helpful to understand what caused an offender's behaviour in order to provide the best rehabilitation. For example, if a person's violence stems from anger, then they may be offered anger management as a treatment.

Psychological formulations can be presented in a diagram, which is easy for professionals working with an offender to digest.

A limitation of psychological formulations is that the psychologist may not have access to all the information about an individual. For example, the offender might not know that they have a brain injury from childhood unless a brain scan is done.

You need to be able to describe and evaluate one cognitive behavioural technique for treating offenders. For example, anger management.

Description:

Anger management is a cognitive-behavioural technique. Anger management programmes are based on the idea that individuals can learn to control their aggression by changing their thought patterns. There are three steps to anger management 1) Cognitive preparation-Offenders are taught to identify situations which trigger anger and thought patterns are challenged 2) Skills acquisition- Offenders are taught skills to control their feelings of anger such as counting to ten and relaxation techniques to calm themselves down 3) Application practice- Offenders are given anger-provoking scenarios such as someone swearing at them so that they can practice how to deal with difficult situations. Anger management programmes can be used in prisons or with people on probation. The courses are usually conducted in small groups and last for around ten sessions.

Evaluation:

Directive-Anger management can be viewed a directive treatment as the therapist has a lot of power and tells the offenders that their thinking is wrong and that they need to change it.

Effectiveness- Dowden, Blanchette and Serin (1999) investigated the effectiveness of an anger management programme in Canada. They found that it was effective at reducing recidivism with high risk offenders over a 3 year period. Goldstein et al. (1989) also found that anger management combined with social skills training could reduce recidivism. However, Watt and Howells (1999) found no difference between offenders who had been through an anger management programme and offenders who had not been treated yet using a range of measures including anger experience, anger expression, prison misconduct and observations of aggressive behaviour. They suggested that the anger management programme had not worked because of the offenders' poor motivation and the limited opportunities to practice the skills learnt. Prisoners may say the programmes are useful simply because they enjoy the break from routine.

Side effects- Anger management programmes do not include a discussion of morality or understanding from a victim's point of view, which has been said to limit their success. Men convicted of domestic violence may become less physically violent after attending an anger management programme but may be more verbally and emotionally abusive.

Expense- Anger management is expensive as it requires highly trained professionals to deliver the programme. It also requires time and commitment from both the prison service and the prisoners as the course requires a number of sessions.

Reasons-Anger management does not uncover any underlying reasons behind the offender's aggression such as childhood issues. It only tries to change present thinking.

Types of people- Anger management works better with offenders who have reactive aggression. It does not work well on offenders whose aggression does not stem from anger. Some offenders use aggression to manipulate others. Watts and Howells (1999) study found that anger management programmes were ineffective but this may be because the offenders were not assessed to see if their aggression was related to anger. Loza and Loza-Fanous (1999) found no link between anger and violent offences.

You need to be able to describe and evaluate one biological treatment for offenders. For example, diet.

Description:

Offenders may suffer from a deficiency in certain vitamins, minerals or essential fatty acids, which leads to increased aggression. This may be because diet can affect hormone levels. Low blood sugar levels have been linked with irritability and this may also lead to aggressive behaviour. Offenders can be given vitamins supplements to address any deficiencies in their diet. They can also be given advice by a dietician about how to eat healthily and how to avoid low blood sugar levels.

Evaluation:

Directive-Offenders may feel under pressure to follow a certain diet.

Effectiveness- Gesch et al. (2002) compared young offenders who were given a dietary supplement to a group of young offenders who were given a placebo. The young offenders who were receiving a supplement showed a 35% reduction in bad behaviour compared to only a 7% reduction amongst the offenders given the placebo. This study supports the idea that a good diet can reduce anti-social behaviour.

Side effects- There are usually no side effects from taking a dietary supplement.

Expense- Employing a dietician or other professional to improve prisoner's diets can be costly.

Reasons-Changing an offender's diet does not address other reasons for the offender's behaviour such as relationship issues.

Types of people- Dietary supplements can be used with most people. Care needs to be taken with pregnant offenders or those with medical issues.

You need to be able to discuss factors influencing eye-witness testimony, (including post-event information and weapon focus).

Post-event information can influence eye-witness testimony. Memory is not like a DVD-recording but instead it is an imaginative reconstruction of events. If there are gaps in our memory, we use schemas to fill in the gaps so that events make sense to us. Leading questions can influence eyewitness memory and produce errors in recall. Loftus and Palmer (1974) found that they could affect participants' recall by changing the way a question was worded. Participants were asked how fast a car was going when it 'hit', 'smashed', 'collided' or 'bumped'. Participants gave a higher estimate of speed if the word was 'smashed' rather than 'collided', they were also more likely to report seeing broken glass in the 'smashed' condition when asked back a week later.

Anxiety levels can also affect recall. Valentine and Mesout (2009) found that participants with high anxiety levels had poorer recall of an actor who stepped in front of them in the London Dungeon.

Studies show that when a weapon is used by a criminal, witnesses focus on the weapon rather than the criminal's face or their environment, probably because a weapon is a major threat. This is called the weapon focus effect. Loftus et al. (1987) showed half of their participants a film with a customer in a restaurant holding a cheque, and the other half were shown a film with a customer holding a gun. They found that participants had worse recall for the customer's face when they were holding a weapon.

If there is a long period of time between recall and the incident, eye-witnesses are likely to forget details.

Stereotypes can affect eyewitness memory. People's views on what type of person commits a crime can affect recall. People are less likely to believe that a man in a suit committed a crime compared to someone who is scruffily dressed.

The memory conformity effect can affect witnesses' memory for events. For example, if witnesses discuss a crime incident together, their memory for events becomes more similar. Wright et al. (2000) placed people in pairs to investigate the memory conformity effect under controlled conditions. One of the pair saw pictures of a man entering with the thief; the other saw pictures without the man. They were then asked to recount the story together but fill out questionnaires separately. About half of the participants who had not seen the picture with the man agreed to their partner's account and said that there was a man entering with a thief.

You need to be able to discuss factors influencing jury decision-making, including characteristics of the defendant and pre-trial publicity. You need to be able to refer to studies.

There are a number of factors that affect jury decision making:

Characteristics of the defendant-Jurors may have stereotyped views about a defendant which influences their reactions. Research suggests that the race and accent of the defendant can affect a jury's decision making. Mahoney and Dixon (1997) found that defendant's with 'Brummie' accents were judged as guiltier than those with standard British accents. In a meta-analysis of 80 studies using mock juries, Mazzella and Feingold (1994) found it was an advantage for a defendant to be physically attractive.

Pre-trial publicity-Jurors may be influenced by media coverage of a high profile case. Fein et al. (1997) used cuttings from the O.J. Simpson case with a mock jury. They found that those who had access to pre-trial publicity were more likely to find the accused guilty.

The foreperson chosen-The foreperson speaks most and is more likely to be white, male and middle aged. Males tend to have less liberal attitudes than women on average. Kerr et al. (1982) found that a disproportionate number of jury forepersons are male and in mixed sex groups, men tend to dominate conversations.

Conformity-One person who is not in agreement with the others is likely to go along with the majority view. Conformity can occur through normative influence, which is the desire to fit in with other members of the group. If a minority of jurors disagree with the majority, they are likely to be presented with a set of persuasive arguments to move them towards the majority view. Group polarisation is when the majority favours one side at the start of a discussion and by the end of it, the majority view is held more strongly. Hastie et al. (1983) found that if at the outset, the majority favoured a guilty verdict, in 90% of cases that was the final outcome.

The size of the jury- In Britain, juries always consist of 12 individuals but in the US juries can be smaller than this. However, evidence suggests larger juries are more effective.

You need to be able to discuss individual differences in criminal and anti-social behaviour including personality as a factor in criminal/anti-social behaviour and individual differences affecting whether a self-fulfilling prophecy occurs.

Individual differences in personality may make people more likely to engage in criminal and anti-social behaviour. Eysenck suggested that high scores for psychoticism, extraversion and neuroticism are linked with criminal and anti-social behaviour. Rushton and Chrisjohn (1981) found a relationship between high extraversion and psychoticism scores and delinquency. Personality disorders are also related to criminal and anti-social behaviour. May violent offenders have anti-social and paranoid personality disorders.

People with low self-esteem are more likely to be affected by other people's negative labels and expectations. Therefore, a self-fulfilling prophecy is more likely to occur with such individuals, which makes them likely to engage in criminal and anti-social behaviour.

You need to be able to discuss social learning theory as a theory of human development that can account for criminal/anti-social behaviour.

Social learning theory suggests people commit crimes because they are exposed to criminal role models. They may look up to a criminal and pay attention to their behaviour. They may remember how the crime is committed and if they are able to carry out the crime themselves (reproduction) and they are motivated to do so, they may commit the same or similar crime themselves (modelling). For example, a boy may observe an older boy stealing cars, he may pay attention to how to do it and be capable of reproducing the behaviour, finally if he identifies with the boy and looks up to him as a role model, he may be motivated to copy the behaviour. Anti-social behaviour can be explained through observation of anti-social role models. The most powerful role models are the same-sex, high status and a similar age to the observer.
If a model is rewarded, a behaviour is more likely to be copied. This is called vicarious reinforcement. For example, if a criminal is successful and becomes rich from their crimes, their behaviour is more likely to be imitated. A criminal such as gang leader may also be rewarded in terms of approval from peers and this also makes their behaviour more likely to be imitated.
However, if the model is punished the behaviour is less likely to be copied. For example, a criminal may be caught and sent to prison for their crimes.

Evaluation of theory:

Use SE to evaluate a theory that has already been applied to criminological psychology.

Studies-What studies support or contradict the theory?

Explanation-What are the problems and limitations of the theory? What alternative explanations are there?

Studies- Bandura, Ross and Ross' (1961) study found that children would copy aggressive behaviour shown by a model so this supports social learning theory. However, this study only looked at whether the children copied the aggressive behaviours soon after rather than whether the children were affected in the long-term. Huesmann and Eron (1986) followed people's viewing habits over 22 years and found that the more violence people watched on TV, the more likely they were to have committed a criminal act by the age of 30. However, correlational studies such as this cannot show a causal relationship as people with a tendency to be antisocial or aggressive may seek out aggressive media. On the other hand, field experiments such as Parke et al. do show a causal link between observed aggression and actual aggression. They carried out a field experiment on boys in an institution for juvenile offenders. One group of boys watched violent TV programmes and one group watched programmes without violence over 5 days. They found that viewing violent TV programmes led to an increase in aggressive behaviour. However, juvenile offenders are not representative of the wider population and may be more prone to aggressive behaviour.

Explanation-It is difficult to establish a causal link between observing criminal or anti-social behaviour and carrying out such behaviour due to the time lapse. Social learning theory does not take into account biological factors in criminal behaviour such as genes, hormones or structural differences in the brain. Another limitation of social learning theory is that it does not consider how social factors such as unemployment and poverty can affect criminality. It also does not explain why many offenders have mental health issues and learning difficulties.

Exam tip: If you use a study to support or contradict a theory, then briefly say what it found and how it supports the theory. You do not need to give a full description of a study in this context, only enough detail so it is recognisable. The examiner only wants to know how the study supports/contradicts the theory. You can make one evaluative point per study used.

Exam tip 2: Do not spend too much time discussing alternative theories. There is often only one mark for this. Instead focus on the limitations and problems of the theory you are evaluating.

You need to be able to discuss biological causes for criminal/anti-social behaviour in relation to development.

Males are most likely to be involved in violent crime between 15 and 25 years old. This may be related to a surge in testosterone levels during this developmental period.

You need to be able to describe and evaluate laboratory experiments in terms of assessing eye-witness effectiveness.

Description:

In a laboratory experiment assessing eye-witness effective, an independent variable such as weapon focus effect or leading questions is manipulated and a dependent variable such as eye-witness recall is measured. For example, in the Loftus and Palmer's (1974) experiment, the independent variable was the verb in the question 'how fast was the car going when it 'hit'/ bumped'/ 'collided'/'smashed.' The dependent variable was participants' estimates of the speed of the car. Laboratory experiments control extraneous variables so that a cause and effect relationship can be established.

Evaluation:

Laboratory experiments are easily replicable as there are good controls over extraneous variables and a standardised procedure is used. In Loftus and Palmer's study, all participants watched the same seven video clips of different traffic accidents and were given the same questionnaire. Loftus and Palmer's study has been replicated several times with the same results, increasing its reliability. Researchers have carried out many laboratory experiments investigating eyewitness effectiveness and have come up with similar findings, which show that the studies are reliable.

Laboratory experiments lack ecological validity as they take place in an artificial setting. For example, Loftus and Palmer's study lacks ecological validity because watching film clips of traffic accidents does not have the same impact or lead to the same emotions as seeing a real life accident and the interview stage would not seem as important as it would if the incident were real. Loftus and Palmer said that the study avoided demand characteristics as the critical questions were randomly hidden amongst others so participants couldn't guess the aim of the study. However, the participants may have felt that they had to give a higher speed estimate when the verb 'smashed' was used so that they didn't come into conflict with the experimenter (experimenter effects).

Laboratory experiments investigating eye-witness recall are likely to require some level of deceit, because the independent variable has to be kept secret so that participants do not deliberately change their behaviour. For example, in the Loftus and Palmer (1974) experiment, the participants might have changed their speed estimates if they knew the researchers were investigating leading questions. As there is some level of deceit required when investigating eyewitness testimony, there is unlikely to be fully informed consent.

You need to be able to describe and field experiments in terms of assessing eye-witness effectiveness.

Description:

Field experiments take place in participants' natural environment and involve manipulating an independent variable. For example, in Yarmey's study a woman approached participants in a public place (a natural environment). A number of independent variables were manipulated such as whether the participants were asked to recall the target immediately or 4 hours later and whether the target wore a disguise or not. In a field experiment, a dependent variable is measured. In Yarmey's study, the researchers measured how many details participants could correctly remember about the woman, whether participants could correctly identify her amongst a set of photos when she was present and whether participants could correctly point out that she was not there in a set of photos where she was absent. As field experiments take place in a natural environment, extraneous variables are not easily controlled although the researcher tries to control as many aspects of the situation as they can.

Maass and Kohnken (1989) carried out a field experiment in which participants were approached by a woman holding either a pen or a syringe. Participants in the 'pen' condition were able to supply more accurate descriptions of the woman. However, this could be due the syringe being an unusual object in the situation rather than because it is a threat. Mitchell et al. (1998) investigated whether people's recall would be affected if someone was holding a celery stick (an unusual object) and they found that it was.

Evaluation:

Field experiments take place in the participants' natural environment. This means that not all the extraneous variables can be controlled and the findings may not be reliable. However, as field experiments have carefully controlled and planned procedures, they often give the same results when repeated. This means that they can be as reliable as laboratory experiments.

Field experiments are carried out in the participants' natural environment so they have ecological validity in terms of setting. However, the independent variable is still carefully manipulated to see the effect on the dependent variable, and therefore, the procedure may not be valid. On the other hand, researchers try to make the procedure as realistic as possible to enhance validity.

Field experiments are often less ethical than laboratory experiments because the participants are approached in public places and often do not know beforehand that they are in a study at all. In field experiments, participants can be asked for their consent afterwards. In Yarmey's study, participants did not know initially that they were part of a study so they did not give consent. The participants were also deceived as the target lied to them about needing help. However, they were told about the study 2 minutes after they met the target. BPS guidelines advise that participants should not be caused distress and that they should leave a study in the same emotional state they started in. Field experiments are more likely to cause a participant distress because the participants do not initially know they are in a study. For example, in the Maass and Kohnken (1989) study, some of the participants were approached in the field by a woman with a syringe. This may have caused the participants distress.

You need to be able to describe and evaluate case studies in terms of assessing eye-witness effectiveness.

Description:

A case study can be carried out if a unique incident or event occurs naturally that might be of interest to the researcher. For example, a natural event could be a real crime and the researchers might want to investigate witnesses' recall of the incident later. For example, in the Yuille and Cutshall study, witnesses observed a real gun shooting and then asked details about the incident later on. Dependent variables can be measured e.g. the number of details recalled accurately about the incident.

Evaluation:

Case studies often take advantage of a naturally occurring incident so they have less ethical issues that field experiments and greater validity. However, they may still involve deception and asking participants to recall a traumatic incident can cause distress. For example, in Yuille and Cutshall's case study participants were deceived about the leading questions. The study could have also caused distress as the participants were asked to recall a gun shooting. On the other hand, participants were given the choice about whether to take part or not.

As case studies often involve a unique incident, they are not replicable and cannot be tested for reliability.

You need to be able to describe and evaluate the classic study: Loftus and Palmer (1974) Reconstruction of automobile destruction: An example of the interaction between language and memory.

Description:

Aim-To see if leading questions affect participants' speed estimates.

Procedure for experiment 1-45 students were put into groups. They watched 7 films of traffic accidents, ranging in duration from 5 to 30 seconds, which were presented in random order to each group. After the film, the participants had to fill in a questionnaire. First they were required to given an account of the accident and then to answer specific questions. The critical question was the one asking about the speed of the vehicles. Nine participants were asked 'about how fast were the cars going when they hit each other?' and equal numbers were asked the same question, but with the word 'hit' being replaced by 'smashed', 'collided' 'bumped' and 'contacted.

Results for experiment 1-They found that if a different verb is used to indicate the speed of a car, such as 'hit', 'smashed', 'collided' or 'bumped', then participants gave a different speed estimate. The highest mean speed estimate was when the verb 'smashed' was used and the lowest mean speed estimate was when the verb 'contacted' was used in the question. There was a 9 mph difference between the speed estimates when the verb 'smashed' was used and when the verb 'contacted' was used.

Conclusion for experiment 1-The wording of a question can affect participants' responses.

Procedure for experiment 2-There were 150 participants involved in this experiment. A 1 minute film with a multiple car accident lasting 4 seconds was shown. After the film, the participants had to give a general account of what they had seen and then answer more specific questions about the accident. 50 participants were asked 'about how fast were the cars going when they hit each other?', another 50 'about how fast were the cars going when they smashed each other?' and another 50 acted as control group who were not asked the question at all. One week later, participants were asked to answer ten questions, one of which was the critical question 'did you see any broken glass? Yes or no?' even though there was no broken glass in the film.

Results for experiment 2-The verb 'smashed' increased the estimate of speed and the likelihood of seeing broken glass even though there was no broken glass. 16/50 participants in the group where the word 'smashed' had been used said they had seen broken glass compared to 7/50 when the word 'hit' had been used and 6/50 in the control group.

Overall conclusion-This study suggests that leading questions can affect recall and lead to distorted memory.
The study questions the reliability of eyewitness testimony and shows that care must be taken when questioning witnesses.

Evaluation:

Generalisability- The study lacks generalisability as all the participants were students who are not representative of the wider population. Students tend to be less experienced drivers and so may have been more easily influenced by the verbs smashed/collided/ contacted etc. in giving their speed estimates.

Reliability-The study had a standardised procedure and good controls. For example, all the participants in experiment 1 watched the same 7 film clips under controlled conditions. This makes the study replicable, and therefore, reliable.

Application to real life- This study suggests that the police should be careful to avoid leading questions when interviewing witnesses. The justice system should also be careful about trusting eyewitness testimony unless it is supported by other corroborating evidence.

Validity-The study lacks ecological validity because the participants lacked the emotional involvement of real eyewitnesses. The participants may have felt correct recall was not as important compared to witnesses of a real crime. The study also used questionnaires, which is nothing like a real police interview.
It could be argued that the study has experimental validity as the critical (leading) questions were all randomly hidden amongst other distractor questions so the participants were not able to guess the aim of the study and so the study avoided demand characteristics. However, others have criticised the study for suffering from experimenter effects as the participants may have felt they had to give a higher speed estimate when the word 'smashed' was used so that they did not come into conflict with the experimenter.
The researchers gathered quantitative data in the form of estimates of speed, which makes the study more objective.

Evidence-Yuille and Cutshall (1986) reported a case of real eyewitness testimony and found that leading questions had little effect on the accuracy of recall even five months after viewing a gun shop robbery. This study contradicts Loftus and Palmer's study.

You need to be able to describe and evaluate one contemporary study in criminological psychology. For example, Valentine T and Mesout J (2009) Eyewitness identification under stress in the London Dungeon.

Description:

Aim-To see whether a situation that causes anxiety and high levels of stress affects eyewitness recall and identification.

Procedure-Visitors to the London Dungeon were offered a reduction in the admission price if they agreed to complete some questionnaires after their visit. 29 female and 27 male volunteers were recruited. Participants were asked to wear a heart rate monitor during their visit. The Horror Labyrinth is the first exhibit in the tour of the London Dungeon and it is designed to scare visitors. During their tour of this section, an actor dressed in a dark robe and wearing theatrical make-up stepped out in front of each participant and blocked their path to prevent them passing. The participant's heart rate was measured using the monitor. At the end of the tour, participants were asked to fill in a questionnaire to measure their state anxiety (how they felt at that moment) and their trait anxiety (their normal level of anxiety). They were also asked to complete a second questionnaire designed to record free recall and cued recall of the scary person. The participants were shown a nine-person photographic line-up and asked to identify the scary person. They were told that the person might or might not be in the line-up. They were then asked to rate their confidence in the decision from 0-100%.

Results-The mean state anxiety score was 49.0. State anxiety was higher for females than for males (52.8 vs. 45.3 respectively). There was no difference in trait anxiety between males and females (36.3 vs. 37.3). People who reported higher state anxiety recalled fewer correct details.
In order to see the effect of state anxiety further, the participants were divided into high and low state anxiety groups based on the median score of 51.5. Participants who reported high state anxiety were less likely to correctly identify the person in the labyrinth. Only 17% of eyewitness who scored above the median on the state anxiety scale correctly identified the person they saw from a nine-person culprit-present photograph line-up. In contrast 75% of eyewitnesses who scored below the median correctly identified the 'culprit'.

Conclusion-Eyewitness identification was dramatically impaired by high state anxiety. Female witnesses may be particularly vulnerable to the effects of stress. The study suggests that the emotional state of witnesses at the time of an incident should be taken into account when considering their testimony.

Evaluation:

Generalisability-All the participants had chosen to visit the London Dungeon. People who choose to visit such a place may be more or less affected by scary situations than average. This means that the sample may not be generalisable to the wider population.

Reliability-The study had good controls and a standardised procedure. All the participants were approached by a scary person at the same point on the tour of the London Dungeon and in the same manner. This makes the study replicable and reliable.

Application to real life-The study suggests that the police and courts should take into account the anxiety level of witnesses when considering the accuracy of their testimony.

Validity- The study has ecological validity as measuring participants' recall of a scary person in the London Dungeon relates to real life witness recall as it was a natural situation. The questionnaires used in to measure state and trait anxiety had previously been shown to be valid.

Ethics-Although the participants were deliberately scared in the study, they had chosen to go to the London Dungeon to experience a scary situation. The participants were told at the end of the tour the purpose of the experiment and given the right to withdraw.

You need to be able to discuss one key question of relevance to today's society, discussed as a contemporary issue for society rather than as an academic argument and apply concepts, theories and/or research to it. For example, 'Is eye-witness testimony too unreliable to trust?'

Eyewitness testimony refers to the recalled memory of a witness to a crime or incident. People have been convicted on the basis of eyewitness testimony alone and have later been found innocent using DNA evidence. Cases like this call into question the reliability of eyewitness testimony. This is an issue as juries place a lot of trust in eyewitness testimony. The police can also distort witnesses' memories by the way they ask questions. Bartlett suggests that people reconstruct their memories so witnesses may fill in the gaps in their memory of an incident using schemas (packets of information about the world). However, witnesses to real life incidents may have a better memory of events due to the strong emotions involved.

Eyewitness Testimony is unreliable because:

Leading questions can influence eyewitness memory and produce errors in recall. Loftus and Palmer (1974) found that they could affect participants' recall by changing the way a question is worded. Participants were asked how fast a car was going when it 'hit', 'smashed', 'collided' or 'bumped'. Participants gave a higher estimate of speed if the word was 'smashed' rather than 'collided', they were also more likely to report seeing broken glass in the 'smashed' condition when asked back a week later.

Anxiety level can affect recall. Valentine and Mesout (2009) found that participants with high anxiety levels had poorer recall of an actor who stepped in front of them in the London Dungeon.

Weapon focus effect: Studies show that when a weapon is used by a criminal, witnesses focus on the weapon rather than the criminal's face or their environment, probably because a weapon is a major threat. Loftus et al. (1987) showed half of their participants a film with a customer in a restaurant holding a cheque, and the other half were shown a film with a customer holding a gun. They found that participants had worse recall for the customer's face when they were holding a weapon.

Yarmey's (2004) study supports the view that jurors should question the reliability of witness identification from line-ups. The found that when participants had actually spoken to a female target, only 49% of them could identify her in a photo line-up when she was present and when she was not present 38% of them identified someone in the photo line-up who was completely different.

Poor line-up procedures may lead to misidentification of a suspect. Simultaneous line-ups (where all the people are presented together in the line-up) may lead to witnesses using a relative judgement strategy (choosing a person who looks most like the perpetrator of the crime rather than really looking at the person's individual characteristics to see whether they match up).

Meissner and Brigham (2001) found that people are less able to recognise people from a different ethnic background to them so this can lead to problems in eyewitness identification.

Buckout (1974) highlighted that photo line-ups can be biased if the suspect's photo is physically different from the fillers.

Busey and Loftus (2006) pointed out that lack of double-blind procedures can mislead witnesses. They gave the example of a police officer who knew who the suspect was in a line-up and when a witness identified the suspect, the police officer said sign here as if to confirm their identification was correct.

Wells and Bradfield (1998) found that if participants were told that their identification of a criminal was correct, they became more confident about their identification. Therefore, by the time a case gets to court, if a witness has had their identification confirmed by a police officer, they may be overly confident even if they are wrong.

If there is a long period of time between recall and the incident, people are likely to forget details.

Stereotypes can affect eyewitness memory. People's views on what type of person commits a crime can affect recall. People are less likely to believe that a man in a suit committed a crime compared to someone who is scruffily dressed.

The memory conformity effect can affect witnesses' memory for events. For example, if witnesses discuss a crime incident together, their memory for events becomes more similar. Wright et al. (2000) placed people in pairs to investigate the memory conformity effect under controlled conditions. One of the pair saw pictures of a man entering with the thief; the other saw pictures without the man. They were then asked to recount the story together but fill out questionnaires separately. About half of the participants who had not seen the picture with the man agreed to their partner's account and said that there was a man entering with a thief.

Eyewitness Testimony is reliable because:

Yuille and Cutshall (1986) examined the recall of witnesses to a real life gun shooting in Canada. 21 witnesses saw a man try to rob a gun shop and then shoot the shop owner. The shop owner shot back and killed the thief. After the witnesses had been interviewed by police, the researcher used the opportunity to ask them whether they would like to take part in the research into eyewitness testimony. 13 of the 21 witnesses agreed to take part in their research 5 months later. They found that even 5 months after the incident, witnesses had good recall of events and were not affected by the leading questions asked. This study suggests that eyewitness memory in real life is not as likely to be distorted as laboratory experiments suggest.

Riniolo et al. (2003) questioned 20 survivors of the shipwrecked Titanic shipwreck and found that 15 of the 20 witnesses were able to recall details accurately many years later despite inaccurate media coverage.

Cognitive interviews can improve eyewitness testimony: this involves getting the witness to freely describe events without the risk of leading questions. Eyewitnesses are asked to not leave out any detail even if they think it is unimportant and they may be asked to recall the incident in reverse order. Questions can be asked at the end in order for information to be un-altered.

Flashbulb memory may lead witnesses to recall crime incidents very clearly as they are likely to have strong emotions related to the incident and may replay events in their mind.

You need to be able to describe and evaluate one practical investigation you have carried out in criminological psychology. Example practical: The effect of leading questions on participant's responses.

Aim-To investigate whether the wording of a question can affect participant's answers

Background research-Loftus and Palmer(1974) carried out a study into the effects of leading questions. The aim of the experiment was to see how recall is affected by the verb used in a question. The procedure involved five groups of students being shown film clips of traffic accidents. Once they had watched the film clips each group was asked the question, 'How fast were the cars travelling when they ....? The last word varied, each group had a different word from the list: contacted, hit, bumped or smashed. The results showed that the group with the verb 'contacted' gave a much lower mean speed estimate of 32 miles per hour compared to 41 miles per hour in the 'smashed' group. This allowed Loftus and Palmer to conclude that simply changing a single word in a sentence can greatly affect the recall of participants or something more important like a witness in court.
Another study looking into leading questions is that of Harris (1973). Participants were shown some basketball players. Some participants were asked 'How tall is the basketball player?' and some were asked, 'How short is the basketball player?'. The results found that when asked 'how short...?' the average answer was 69 inches compared to the 79 inches estimated when asked 'how tall...?

Directional hypothesis- Participants who are asked the question 'How long is this piece of string?' will give a longer estimate compared to participants who are asked the question 'How short is this piece of string?'

Null hypothesis- There will be no difference in participants' estimates of the length of string whether they are asked the question 'How long is this piece of string?' or 'How short is this piece of string?'

Research Method-A laboratory experiment was used so a cause an effect relationship could be established. The independent variable was the question 'How short is this piece of string?'/'How long is this piece of string?' The dependent variable was the estimated length of the string. Extraneous variables were kept the same (the piece of string, the environment).

Design-An independent group design was used so that each participant only experienced one condition (one of the two questions). This was to avoid demand characteristics.

Sample-An opportunity sample of 24 participants was recruited from friends and family. There were an equal number of males and females and their age ranged from 18 to 80 years old.

Procedure-Participants were approached individually and asked to take part in an experiment on eyewitness testimony. They were briefed on the experiment and what it would involve. They were shown the piece of string and the first twelve participants were asked, 'How short is this piece of string?'. The second twelve participants were asked, 'How long is this piece of string?' Their answers were noted down in a notepad. Participants were debriefed afterwards and given the right to withdraw.
A table to show the difference in recall when asked 'How long is this piece of string?' compared to the recall when asked 'How short is this piece of string?'

	RECALL WHEN ASKED HOW LONG? (CM)	RECALL WHEN ASKED HOW SHORT? (CM)
MODE	43	31
MEAN	43.6	31.8
MEDIAN	44	31
RANGE	7	8

Results-There was a significant difference between the sets of results. The group asked 'How long is this piece of string?' estimated a mean length of 43.6cm while the group asked 'How short is this piece of string?' estimated a mean length of 31.8cm. This is a difference of 11.8cm. This is a significant enough difference to allow me to accept my directional hypothesis (that those asked 'How long...?' will give a longer estimate).

Conclusion-People are affected by leading questions. There was a significant difference in participants' length estimates when asked 'How long is this piece of string?' compared to 'How short is this piece of string?'

Evaluation-As this experiment is a laboratory experiment, it lacks ecological validity as people are not usually asked to estimate the length of string in real life. It is not the same as being asked questions about a witnessed incident by the police or in court.

An opportunity sample was used, which makes it difficult for somebody else to get the same type of sample and makes the study less reliable. However, there was good control over extraneous variables which makes the study easier to replicate and increases the reliability.

It is hard to generalise from an opportunity sample to the wider population. However, a large age range was used, which makes the study more generalisable.

You need to be able to describe ethical issues in criminological psychology

Psychologists need to be careful that they do not cause distress to participants when investigating eyewitness effectiveness and jury decision-making as these can involve mock trials and fake crime incidents. Experiments looking at factors affecting eyewitness testimony can involve deception so it is important that participants are protected from psychological harm and thoroughly debriefed at the end. Field experiments where participants do not know that they are part of an experiment initially need to be particularly careful to avoid causing harm.

You need to know practical issues in the design and implementation of research

Field experiments take place in participants' natural environment so they have good ecological validity. They are a useful research method as the participants' behaviour will be more like real witnesses compared to participants in laboratory experiments, who are engaged in artificial tasks in an artificial setting. In a field experiment, participants often do not know initially that they are part of a study, so their attention to the environment will be similar to real witnesses. For example, in Yarmey's study the participants did not pay particular attention to a target woman when she approached them asking for directions or help finding a lost piece of jewellery. In contrast, laboratory experiments involve asking witnesses to focus their attention on a film clip or slides of an incident. Therefore, laboratory experiments lack ecological validity. A weakness of field experiments is a lack control over the extraneous variables, which makes them less reliable than laboratory experiments. On the other hand, this lack of control over the extraneous variables makes field experiments more like a real incident.

You need to be able to discuss reductionism in criminological psychology

Criminological psychologists often reduce criminal behaviour down to single factors such as genes, relationships or environment in order to explain it. When psychologists consider only one influence on criminal behaviour at a time, then this is reductionist as it does not take into account all the factors that affect criminality.

You need to be able to compare different ways of explaining criminal behaviour

Both social learning theory and the self-fulfilling prophecy suggest that criminality is affected by other people's behaviour. However, social learning theory suggests that criminal behaviour occurs through observing others whereas the self-fulfilling prophecy proposes that it occurs as a result of other people's expectations.
Social learning theory would say criminal behaviour runs in families due to the role models provided by parents whereas the biological approach would explain it as a result of genes.

You need to be able to discuss whether criminological psychology is a science

Laboratory experiments in criminological psychology such as Loftus and Palmer's study on leading questions are scientific because they control extraneous variables and establish cause and effect relationships. Field experiments have less control over extraneous variables and are therefore less scientific. However, both types of experiment collect quantitative data, which is objective and can be statistically analysed.

When interviews or case studies are used, the data is more subjective and less scientific.

You need to be able to discuss cultural issues in criminological psychology

Stereotypes can influence eyewitnesses and juries. The legal system needs to be aware of how cultural factors affect witness recall and jury decision making. For example, accent can influence whether someone is found guilty and race can affect witness recall of an incident.

You need to be able to discuss gender in criminological psychology

Most research in criminological psychology focuses on male offenders. Therefore, findings from such research cannot be generalised to female offenders.

You need to be able to discuss the nature-nurture debate in criminological psychology

The nature side of the debate would argue that criminal behaviour is caused by biological factors such as genes, hormones and brain structure. The nurture side of the debate would argue that criminal behaviour is affected by environmental factors such as family background and role models. Twin studies show that MZ twins have a higher concordance rate for anti-social behaviour than DZ twins. However, as the concordance is not 100%, this suggests that environmental factors influence anti-social behaviour too.

You need to be able to discuss how psychological understanding has developed over time in criminological psychology

James Cattell carried out the first research into eyewitness testimony in 1893. He found that although people might be confident in their answers they weren't always correct. His research led to a wealth of research into the inaccuracy of eyewitness testimony. Psychologists started to be used as experts in court to explain the problems with witnesses' memories. More recently, brain scans have been used to understand differences in the brain functioning of criminals.

You need to be able to discuss how psychological knowledge has been used in criminological psychology

Research on eyewitness testimony has led to reforms in the way witnesses are questioned. For example, the cognitive interview technique has been developed to improve eyewitness testimony and there have been changes in the way line-ups are conducted. Studies looking at jury decision-making have led to a better understanding of how race, accent and social class affect jurors' judgements.

You need to discuss issues related to socially sensitive research in criminological psychology

Research looking at how genes and brain structure affect criminal behaviour can be considered socially sensitive as it could identify individuals who are more likely to commit a crime. It also has implications for society in terms of whether offenders are responsible for their actions.

You need to be able to discuss issues of social control in criminological psychology

Treatments used with offenders can be seen as a form of social control. For example, Token Economy Programmes (TEPs) are used in prisons to control behaviour but research suggests that they don't change behaviour long-term. Other treatments such as anger management are more likely to prevent re-offending once a person leaves the prison environment.

Using psychological research, explain whether courts should rely on eyewitness testimony. You must evaluate eyewitness testimony research in you answer. (12 marks)

Student answer:

Some studies suggest that eyewitness testimony is unreliable. Loftus and Palmer found that when they used a verb that had more force behind it (i.e. smashed compared with bumped) participants gave higher speed estimates. These results from this study suggest that courts should be careful with eyewitness testimony as it isn't completely reliable.

Other studies such as Yuille and Cutshall found that participants who were real life participants weren't affected by leading questions or by the time lapse of five months after the incident had happened. This study suggests that eyewitness testimony is not completely unreliable and shouldn't be disregarded.

The two studies above create a small problem as they contradict each other. However, Yuille and Cutshall's study used real life witnesses whereas Loftus and Palmer used students from a university who watched video clips. There is a big difference as participants watching the video clips may feel that their statements won't matter as much as it isn't real life; compared to real life witnesses who have been affected by the incident and their statement can affect another person's life. Bartlett's theory of reconstructive memory is crucial to understanding eyewitness testimony. He suggests that recall is subject to personal interpretation that is dependent on our culture, values and the way we make sense of the world. When we store things in our memory, we do so in the way that makes most sense to us using schemas. Therefore, memories can be distorted and courts should be cautious about the accuracy of eyewitness testimony.

There are other factors that can affect a person's memory of an incident, for example the media has a major influence. If the incident is covered in the media, eyewitnesses may pay attention to the story and find themselves believing the story given.

In the past, there have been cases where people are convicted due to eyewitness evidence given in court but later found innocent. The research suggests that some other evidence (i.e. forensic or physical) other than eyewitness testimony should be present to convict a person of a crime.

Laboratory experiments are easily replicable as there is a standardised procedure and good controls over extraneous variables. Therefore, laboratory experiments investigating eyewitness testimony are reliable. However, laboratory experiments can lack ecological validity. Getting participants to watch film clips or slides of an incident does not lead to the same emotions as watching a real life incident. Therefore, participants may not respond in the same way as real witnesses. Participants in a laboratory experiment may also not place the same importance as real witnesses on recalling events accurately.

Field experiments are less reliable than laboratory experiments as not all the extraneous variables can be controlled. However, researchers do try to control the extraneous variables as much as possible so field experiments into eyewitness testimony can be reliable. Field experiments often have greater ecological validity as they are carried out in participants' natural environment. For example, if participants see a fake robbery in a public place, they are likely to experience the same emotions as real witnesses.

8/12 marks-level 3 answer

Commentary:

This answer does not refer to enough psychological research. More studies should be given related to whether eyewitness testimony is accurate or not. You should know at least three studies related to eyewitness testimony in detail but it is better to know more in order to answer this type of question.
The second part of the question is asking for an evaluation of eyewitness testimony research more generally. This student makes a good attempt at discussing the validity and reliability of both laboratory and field experiments as used to investigate eyewitness testimony. They could have highlighted that the independent variable(s) is still carefully manipulated in a field experiment and so the procedure can lack validity. There could also have been some discussion of ethical issues. Field experiments have more ethical issues than laboratory experiments because setting up fake crimes in the field or fake car crashes can be more distressing than watching film clips or slides of an incident as is often the case in laboratory experiments.

Chapter 3 - Issues and debates

Key Debates

The Nature-Nurture Debate

The nature-nurture debate refers to the controversy over whether we are born to think, feel and behave in a certain way or whether we learn it from our environment. The nature side of the argument says that our behaviour is determined from birth. The biological approach is the main supporter of nature side of the debate. It focuses on how our genes, nervous system, brain structure and hormones affect our behaviour. It used research methods such as twin and adoption studies, DNA studies and brain scans to study the effects of genes and brain structure on behaviour. The biological approach promotes treatments such as drug therapy, electroconvulsive therapy and brain surgery because it believes that behaviour is changed only through physical means. Twin and adoption studies have been carried out to demonstrate a genetic basis for behaviour.

The nurture side of the debate suggests that we learn all our behaviour from our environment. The learning approach supports the nurture side of the debate as it says that we learn behaviour through classical conditioning, operant conditioning and social learning. The learning approach has used experiments to show how children can learn behaviours from their environment. For example, Watson and Rayner classically conditioned little Albert to be afraid of a white rat he was originally unafraid of. Bandura, Ross and Ross (1961) found that children would copy aggressive behaviour shown by an adult role model to a plastic bobo doll. Such studies support the idea that we learn behaviour from our environment.

However, behaviour is likely to be a mixture of both nature and nurture. For example, a child may be born with a genetic predisposition to have a high IQ but they will only develop a high IQ if they are exposed to a stimulating environment and have a good education.

The debate over whether psychology a science

There is a debate over whether psychology is a science. This may be because there are different approaches within psychology. Some approaches such as the learning approach and biological approach are more scientific and use well, controlled laboratory experiments to collect objective, quantitative data. They use theories to develop hypotheses, which are then tested to see whether they are supported or not by empirical evidence. These approaches aim to build a body of scientific knowledge from the data collected. In contrast, other approaches in psychology such as the psychodynamic approach are less scientific as they use cases studies and interviews, which are open to interpretation. Some approaches such as the cognitive and the social approach are scientific in some ways but not others. The cognitive approach uses controlled laboratory experiments to investigate memory and forgetting. However, the operationalisation of the variables in experiments may lead to problems with validity. For example, learning and recalling a list of words may not be a valid way of testing memory. The cognitive approach also has concepts that are less scientific such as schema, which are difficult to test. The social approach uses laboratory experiments to investigate obedience and prejudice, which are scientific. However, it also uses interviews and field studies to gather data, which can be subject to bias and are less scientific.

The debate over whether animals should be used in psychological research

It could be argued that animals should be used in research to ease human suffering and that we should have more sympathy for our own species than other species. Another argument is that animals do not have the same feelings or experience the same pain as humans. Therefore, we should use animals in preference to humans for research. There are also strict laws and codes of conduct that protect animals used in research which minimises animal suffering. Less invasive methods are used where possible to study animal behaviour.

A problem with using animals in research is that it is difficult to generalise the findings to humans as we are more complex. The human brain is different to animals, for example, we have consciousness and can imagine what others are thinking. Research shows that animals can suffer distress, pain and anxiety. Therefore, we should not use animals on moral grounds.

Key Issues

Cultural issues in psychological research

Ethnocentrism can occur if we interpret research findings or people's behaviour entirely through the lens of our own culture without taking into account cultural differences. This can lead to cultural bias. For example, researchers may not take into account the beliefs, customs or language of people from a different culture when conducting research and interpreting findings. The vast majority of psychological research has been carried out in the USA by white, middle class, males which can create bias in the interpretation of findings. If the findings of studies conducted in the USA are generalised to all cultures, this can be seen as ethnocentric. For example, views about the signs and symptoms of mental disorders in DSM may be ethnocentric. However, DSM-V tries to overcome cultural issues in diagnosis by describing how people from different cultures talk about mental health issues differently.

Cross-cultural research

Cross-cultural research refers to researchers repeating studies in different countries/cultures to see if a theory is universal and can explain human behavior across all cultures. Cross-cultural research on obedience has been carried out. For example, Milgram's study has been repeated in other countries with similar results. This suggests that people have similar obedience levels in other countries.

There has also been cross-cultural research on attachment types using the Strange Situation. Ainsworth's classification of different attachment types has been criticised for being culturally biased. However, research has found that type B (secure) attachments are the most common across all cultures. This suggests that the strange situation procedure is a useful tool for assessing attachment type across all cultures. Van Ijzendoorn and Kroonenberg (1988) compared the results of 32 cross-cultural studies and found that there were differences in the proportions of different attachment types in different cultures. However, type B (secure) attachments were the most common type of attachment in all the studies from different cultures, with the exception of one study from Germany. Interestingly, there were more differences in attachment types within a culture compared to between cultures.

How can cultural bias be reduced?

By taking into account a culture's customs and norms before interpreting the results of studies. For example, it is important to take Japanese culture into account before deciding that more children in Japan have insecure resistant attachments. Miyake et al. (1985) found that Japanese infants had a higher proportion of resistant attachments but this may be due to Japanese mothers rarely leaving their children with anyone else and encouraging dependency.

Issues related to the use of psychological knowledge as a means of social control

Psychology has been used to get people to conform to the rules and norms of society. This is called social control.

Psychological therapies can be used to control people so that they conform to society's norms. If therapies are being used to control people rather than help them then this raises ethical issues. Furthermore, if professionals delivering therapies have too much power then this is an ethical issue to. Sometimes people who are a danger to themselves or others due to mental health reasons are forcibly brought to a psychiatric institution under the Mental Health Act. Society needs to be careful that the rights of the individual are not infringed in these circumstances. However, it could be argued that we need social control so that people can live in society safely without fear of harm.

Ethical Issues in psychological research with humans

When psychologists carry out research they have two considerations in mind: the benefit to the society and psychological understanding and the costs in terms of possible harm to the participants. This is called an ethical dilemma.

Psychologists need to adhere to the following ethical guidelines when carrying out research:

Distress-Participants should be protected from psychological or physical harm. The risk of harm should be no greater than that found in everyday life.

Informed Consent-Participants should be provided with enough information about the aim of the study and the procedure so that they can make an informed choice about whether to take part or not.

Deception-Participants should not be deceived about the aim of the study or the procedure. If deception is unavoidable, then permission should be sought from the British Psychological Society.

Debriefing-Participants should be fully informed of the purpose and expected outcomes of the study after they have taken part.

Right to withdraw-Participants should be told that they are free to leave the study at any time and they have the right to remove their results at the end, regardless of any payment they have received.

Confidentiality-Participants' should be guaranteed anonymity and their data should be stored securely.

Ethical Issues in animal experiments

Animals are only used in experiments when there is a clear benefit to the research. Bateson's cube can be used to determine whether the research should go ahead. Bateson's cube has 3 edges labelled; quality of research, animal suffering and certainty of medical benefit. These are on a scale high to low. When a research proposal falls into the opaque region, experiment should not be conducted i.e. when quality of research is low, animal suffering is high and certainty of benefit is low.

The following ethical guidelines need to be followed when carrying out research on animals:

Caging and Stress-Experimenters should avoid or minimise stress and suffering for all living animals. The cages the animals are kept in during the experiment should be large enough for the animals to be comfortable.

Number or animals used-Researchers should use as few animals as possible.

Wild Animals-Endangered species should not be used, unless the research has direct benefits for that species e.g. conservation.

Qualified Experimenters-The researchers conducting the experiment should have the necessary qualifications. They should also have a licence from the Home office for that particular experiment.

Look for alternatives-Alternatives to using animals must always be sought, such as using humans or computers.

Social Psychology

You need to be able to discuss ethics when researching obedience and prejudice in social psychology

Milgram's studies on obedience can be considered unethical as they did not protect participants from psychological harm. Contemporary studies on obedience such as Burger (2009) have aimed to investigate obedience whilst protecting participants from harm. The problem with obedience research is that it is difficult to study obedience without deceiving participants. When participants are ordered to harm another person as in much obedience research, the participants are going to be at risk of psychological harm.

Studies on prejudice can also cause psychological harm to participants especially when groups are put in competition with each other. For example, Sherif's study caused conflict between two groups of boys at a summer camp. In this study, the boys were also deceived.

It is questionable whether the findings from obedience and prejudice research are important enough to justify the deception and psychological harm caused.

You need to be able to discuss practical issues in the design and implementation of research in social psychology

One practical issue with obedience research is demand characteristics. Participants may guess the aim of an experiment and change their behaviour. Milgram told participants that he was looking at the effects of punishment on learning rather than obedience to prevent demand characteristics. He also used a confederate and a fake electric shock machine to deceive participants and avoid demand characteristics.

A practical issue with prejudice research is that people are unlikely to admit to being prejudiced in questionnaires and interviews as this is not socially desirable. Questionnaires need to be designed carefully in order to assess prejudiced attitudes. One way to see whether a questionnaire is valid is to assess whether participants respond in the same way to questions that are worded differently but are asking the same thing.

You need to be able to discuss reductionism in social psychology

Reductionism refers to explaining complex human behaviour in terms of simpler elements. Social psychology aims to understand human behaviour in social situations without being reductionist. However, there are some theories within the social approach that are reductionist. For example, social impact theory describes how people are influenced by others in social situations and reduces it to a formula: impact = function of (strength of the sources x immediacy of sources x number of sources). Reducing social impact down to a mathematical formula may be too simplistic a way of understanding how people are influenced by others as there are so many different factors involved. The theory also ignores individual differences in obedience such as having a non-conformist personality.

You need to be able to make comparisons between ways of explaining behaviour using different themes

Realistic conflict theory and social identity theory both refer to in-groups and out-groups when describing prejudice. However, realistic conflict theory focuses on how competition over resources can lead to prejudice whereas social identity theory says that the mere existence of another group can lead to prejudice.

Agency theory and social impact theory explain obedience differently. Agency theory says we have evolved to be obedient as this helps maintain a stable society. It also says that we are socialised in childhood to be obedient. In contrast, social impact theory focuses on the social conditions required for obedience such as how close the authority figures are to us.

You need to be able to discuss social psychology as a science

Experimental social psychology is scientific. For example, Milgram carried out his studies on obedience in a laboratory setting and Tajfel et al. (1971) investigated prejudice under controlled conditions. However, some aspects of social psychology are less scientific. For example, when unstructured interviews are used find out about people's opinions, feelings and experiences they can be subject to interpretation.

You need to be able to discuss cultural issues in social psychology

Culture may have an impact on obedience. For example, collectivist cultures may value obedience more than individualistic cultures. However, research into obedience in other cultures suggests that variations in obedience may be to do with how the studies were carried out rather than cultural differences. For example, Ancona and Paryeson (1968) found a higher obedience rate in Italy but they only used 330V as their maximum shock level.

You need to be able to discuss gender issues in social psychology

Gender stereotypes might suggest that females would be more obedient than males to authority figures. However, research by Milgram and others have found no significant differences in obedience levels between males and females.

You need to be able to discuss the nature-nurture debate in social psychology

Research into prejudice has looked at whether it is cause by dispositional factors (nature) or situational factors (nurture). Adorno et al. suggest that prejudice is related to having an authoritarian personality type. People who are status orientated, conventional and right-wing are more likely to be prejudiced. Therefore, the theory emphasises the nature side of the debate. However, authoritarian personality theory also suggests that parenting style (an environmental factor) affects personality. Social identity theory and realistic conflict theory focus on situational factors in prejudice. Both theories argue that prejudice is related to stereotypes in society and group membership so they support the nurture side of the debate.

You need to be able to show an understanding of how psychological knowledge had developed over time in social psychology

Research in social psychology is influenced by changes in society and important events. For example, the Holocaust led to research on obedience. Riots have led to research into crowd behaviour. More recently, research has been carried out looking at people's experiences on social networking sites.

You need to be able to discuss issues of social control in social psychology

Research on obedience can be used to control people. For example, the military could use such psychological knowledge to train soldiers to be unquestioningly obedient. However, social control can be positive as well. Research into obedience can be used to train people to avoid blind obedience. For example, nurses can be trained to question doctor's orders if they think it may cause the patient harm.

You need to be able to discuss the use of social psychological knowledge in society

Sherif et al.'s study showed how prejudice could be reduced by getting groups to work towards a superordinate goal (a goal that can only be achieved by working together). Other research has shown how education and equal status contact can reduce prejudice. Gaertner et al. found that combining intergroup contact with cooperative interaction is particularly effective at reducing prejudice. They interviewed 1,300 pupils at a multicultural American high school and found that pupils who had engaged in the most cooperative interaction were the least prejudiced.

You need to be able to discuss issues related to socially sensitive research in social psychology

Sieber and Stanley define socially sensitive research as: 'Studies in which there are potential consequences or implications, either directly for the participants in the research or for the class of individuals represented by the research'. Research looking at group behaviour has the potential to be socially sensitive. For example, a study looking at prejudiced attitudes to immigration might perpetuate prejudiced views. Psychologists also need to consider where the funding for their research is coming from and how their research will be used. For example, funding for the Zimbardo prison simulation experiment came from the military. Research could be used by the military as a form of social control. Psychologists need to consider whether their research can be used to restrict individual choice.

Cognitive Psychology

You need to be able to discuss ethical issues in cognitive psychology

Experiments investigating memory tend to follow BPS ethical guidelines and rarely cause psychological harm. However, some research does deceive participants and it is important that participants are fully debriefed and given the right to withdraw at the end. Case studies of brain-damaged patients can be criticised for subjecting vulnerable individuals to intensive testing and violating their right to privacy. However, the patients' anonymity is ensured by giving them pseudonyms.

You need to be able to discuss practical issues in the design and implementation of research in cognitive psychology

A practical issue with memory research is that many experiments lack ecological validity as they are often conducted in artificial settings. Testing memory using lists of words or trigrams does not reflect how we use memory in real life and so the tasks lack mundane realism.

You need to be able to discuss reductionism in cognitive psychology

Many memory theories reduce memory down to separate parts. For example, the multi-store model of memory reduces memory down to sensory memory, short-term memory and long-term memory without taking into account the interactions between each memory store. More recently brain scans have shown the interactions between different brain regions when processing information.

You need to be able to compare different explanations of memory in cognitive psychology

The multi-store model of memory is more simplistic than the working memory model as it suggests that we only have three memory stores: sensory memory, short-term memory (STM) and long-term memory (LTM). It is now widely believed that both STM and LTM have several separate storage systems. The working memory model argues that there are separate short-term memory systems to handle visual and verbal information.

Both the multi-store model of memory and the working memory model focus on the idea of memory consisting of different stores. Therefore, they are both structural models of memory. There are other theories of memory that emphasise information processing rather than structure. The levels of processing theory of memory says we remember information better if we process it deeply rather than at a shallow level. Bartlett's reconstructive theory of memory focuses on how we construct memories using schemas.

You need to be able to discuss cognitive psychology as a science

The cognitive approach often uses experimental methods to investigate topics such as memory and forgetting. Laboratory experiments have good controls and are able to establish cause and effect relationships. This makes such research more scientific. Therefore, the cognitive approach is considered one of the more scientific approaches in psychology.

You need to able to discuss the nature nurture debate in cognitive psychology

The cognitive approach supports the nature side of the debate because it believes that we are born with certain structures such as short-term memory and long-term memory that allow us to process information. However, it also believes that our environment (nurture) affects our cognitive functioning. For example, our schema are affected by our experiences.

You need to be able to discuss how psychological knowledge has developed over time in cognitive psychology

In the 1880s, Ebbinghaus used experiments to study memory. He suggested that there are three types of memory: sensory, short-term and long-term. Bartlett's research in the 1930s led to the theory of reconstructive memory and has influenced later ideas on how the brain stores information.

In the 1950s and 1960s, psychologists started to compare computer processes with how the human brain process information. The led to advances in the understanding of encoding, storage and retrieval.

In 1968, Atkinson and Schiffrin developed the multi-store model of memory, which became the popular model for studying memory for many years although it is now viewed as overly simplistic. Tulving elaborated on the nature of long-term memory in 1972 by making a distinction between episodic and semantic memory. In 1974, Baddeley and Hitch proposed the working memory model, which gave a better explanation for short-term memory. The episodic buffer was added to this model in 2000 to explain how the different components of the model could integrate information.

You need to be able to discuss the use of psychological knowledge from the cognitive approach within society

Memory research has helped psychologists explain some of the memory problems which people with anterograde amnesia have and to develop appropriate therapies. Understanding memory has also helped in the treatment of people with Alzheimers. The concept of working memory can be helpful in understanding the difficulties that children with dyslexia face. Working memory is important in reading and understanding words and so deficits in working memory can lead to the problems in these areas. Many children with dyslexia can also have difficulties with following a sequence of instructions and focusing their attention. Understanding that children with dyslexia may find it difficult to do a number of different things at the same time can inform teaching practice.

The theory of reconstructive memory has been used to explain why eyewitness testimony can be inaccurate. Research into the effect of leading questions, weapon focus effect, memory conformity effect and anxiety on witnesses has led to improvements in the legal system. The police use cues to aid witnesses' recall of incidents during interviews and avoid leading questions.

Biological Psychology

You need to be able to discuss ethical issues in biological psychology

Animals have been used to investigate biological aspects of behaviour. However, there are ethical issues in using animals in research. For example, Rechstaffen et al (1983) aimed to see the effects of sleep deprivation on rats. In this laboratory experiment, researchers placed rats on a disc above a bucket of water. When the rats fell asleep the disc would rotate and in order to not fall into the water, the rats had to stay awake and walk on the disc. The rats eventually died after severe sleep deprivation. It is questionable whether there is any clear benefit to this research and it certainly caused the rats to suffer distress and die. One ethical guideline for animal research says that experimenters should avoid or minimise stress and suffering for all living animals, which was not done in this study.

There are ethical issues with some studies using humans as well. For example, in Li et al.'s study, the heroin addicts were shown heroin related images and this might have triggered a desire to use the drug, which is unethical. PET scans have been used to highlight areas of brain activity and to identify parts of the brain that are not functioning normally. However, they require a patient to be injected with a radioactive substance, which although low risk could have potentially harmful effects if done too many times.

You need to be able to discuss practical issues in the design and implementation of research in biological psychology

Twin and adoption studies have been used in biological psychological to establish a genetic basis for behaviour. An assumption with twin studies is that MZ twins and DZ twins share similar environments and the only difference between MZ twins and DZ twins is that MZ twins share 100% of their genes whereas DZ twins share 50% of their genes. However, this assumption can be questioned. MZ twins are often treated more similarly than DZ twins, for example, they are often dressed the same and people may respond to them in similar ways because they look the same. Therefore, it may be the more similar experiences of MZ twins rather than genes, which leads to them having higher concordance rates for IQ, personality characteristics and mental disorders. Studying separated twins makes it easier to assess the influence of genes versus environment. However, separated twins may still have shared the same environment for a certain amount of time before separation. Another problem with twin studies is that most people are not twins so it is hard to generalise from twins to the wider population.

A problem with adoption studies is that adoption agencies usually try to place children in families that are similar to the biological family. Therefore, it is difficult to separate out the influence of genes and the environment. Furthermore, most people are not adopted so it is hard to generalise findings from adoptees to the wider population.

Brains scans are used in biological psychology to look at the function of different brain regions. They are considered to be a scientific method but researchers still have to make inferences about what certain brain regions are used for and so the results need to be treated with caution. In Raine et al.'s study, differences in brain activity were found between the murderers and the non-murderers but we cannot be certain that the murderers had these differences before they carried out the murder. It is possible that changes in brain activity occurred as a consequence of carrying out their crime. Furthermore, environmental factors such as a poor home life may have led to the differences in brain activity and the violent behaviour rather than biological factors.

You need to be able to discuss reductionism in biological psychology

Biological psychology reduces behaviour down to genes, brain structure and the nervous system. However, most psychologists believe that human behaviour is affected by the interaction of genes and environment. For example, genetic factors may influence aggression but so does growing up with aggressive role models.

You need to be able to discuss biological psychology as a science

The biological approach is considered scientific as it usually collects data from controlled experiments. It uses theories to develop hypotheses, which are then tested to see whether they are supported or not by empirical evidence. Therefore the biological approach is able to build a body of scientific knowledge from the data collected. The biological approach also uses brains scans to understand more about how the brain works. However, inferences are made from brain scans which may not be valid. Twin studies and adoption studies try to establish genetic links for mental disorders and developmental disorders. However, twin and adoption studies are correlational and cannot separate out the influence of genes from the environment.

You need to be able to discuss the nature-nurture debate in biological psychology

The biological approach mainly supports the nature side of the debate. It says that we are born with certain genes and a nervous system that affect the way we think, feel and behave. However, the biological approach accepts that our environment, for example, our diet can affect our development.

You need to be able to show an understanding of how psychological knowledge has developed over time

In 1859, Charles Darwin introduced ideas about natural selection and evolution. This led to link between genetic inheritance and behaviour. In 1861, Paul Broca showed that brain damage affected language and behaviour by studying a man who had suffered a brain injury. William James argued in 1890 that psychology should be grounded in an understanding of biology. Twin studies and adoption studies have been used to investigate the effect of genetics on behaviour. Advances in brain scanning techniques have given us a better understanding of how brain structure and brain activity affect behaviour. For example, Raine et al. (1997) used PET scans to look at the differences in brain activity between murderers and non-murderers.

You need to be able to discuss issues of social control in biological psychology

When biological understanding is used to control behaviour then this is a form of social control. An example of this is when drugs are given to people who have committed an offence in order to change their behaviour. For example, sex offenders have been given drugs which reduce their male hormone levels and hence their sexually deviant behaviour. Some people argue that this is a good use of biological knowledge whereas others feel it is unethical.
Research into aggression could be used to control people in our society. For example, those who are identified as at risk of aggression as a result of brain scans or genetic testing might have some of their rights taken away.

You need to be able to discuss the use of psychological knowledge from the biological approach

The biological approach has contributed to our understanding of aggression by explaining it in terms of biological concepts. Understanding that aggression has a biological basis can take the blame away from the individual and has implications for society. Raine et al compared the brains of murderers and non-murderers using PET scans and found that the 41 murderers who were pleading not guilty by reason of insanity had lower activity in the prefrontal cortex, parietal cortex and corpus callosum than the non-murderers. Such findings can affect the type of sentencing given.

You need to be able to discuss issues related to socially sensitive research in biological psychology

Research showing a biological basis for aggression is socially sensitive as it has implications for society. If biological factors are involved in aggression, it suggests that individuals are not responsible for their actions. This leads to the question of whether people should be criminalised for behaviour that is outside of their control. It also means that biological markers can be used to identify those people who are at risk of aggressive behaviour and some groups might want to control those individuals as a preventative measure. This is an ethical issue.

Learning Theories

You need to be able to discuss ethical issues related to learning theories

Animal experiments have been used in the learning approach to investigate behaviour and many of these studies have ethical issues. For example, Skinner gave electric shocks to rats to investigated negative reinforcement. Ethical guidelines now say that experimenters should avoid or minimise stress and suffering for all living animals.
There have also been ethical issues in experiments involving humans. For example, Watson and Rayner (1920) conditioned a fear response in a baby boy, Little Albert. This experiment caused Little Albert psychological distress, which goes against ethical guidelines.

You need to be able to discuss practical issues in the design and implementation of research related to learning theories

Humans are more complex than animals and so it is difficult to generalise results from animal studies to humans. The human brain functions in a different way to animals.

A problem with using humans to investigate learning theories is that they are likely to show demand characteristics.

You need to be able to discuss reductionism in relation to learning theories

The theories of classical conditioning and operant conditioning are reductionist because they reduce behaviour down to learned responses. Social learning theory is less reductionist because it takes into account cognitive factors (thought processes) in behaviour as well as learned responses.

You need to be able to make comparisons between different learning theories

Classical conditioning, operant conditioning and social learning theory explain how we learn behaviour from our environment. However, classical conditioning focuses on learning through association, operant conditioning focuses on learning through consequences and social learning theory focuses on learning through observation. The different theories can be applied to different aspects of behaviour. For example, classical conditioning is useful at explaining how we might learn a phobia, operant conditioning is useful at explaining how desired behaviour can be reinforced and social learning theory is useful at explaining the impact of role models.

You need to be able to discuss psychology as a science and learning theories

Learning theories have been developed using a scientific approach. Research in this area has tried to measure responses to certain stimuli using objective, empirical evidence from laboratory experiments. For example, Skinner measured how often a rat would press a lever when given rewards.

You need to be able to discuss cultural issues in relation to learning theories

Learning theories focus on environmental influences on behaviour. Culture is one of the environmental influences that play an important part in how we behave. For example, some cultures are more accepting of aggression than others.

You need to be able to discuss gender issues in relation to learning theories

Learning theories emphasise that gender differences are caused by environmental influences from parents, school, society, peers, TV and other models.

Operant conditioning can be used to explain gender differences. Gender-appropriate behaviour is encouraged from birth and gender-stereotypical behaviours are reinforced. For example, girls may be encouraged to play with dolls and boys with cars. Gender-inappropriate behaviours are punished. For example, when boys play with dolls they may be laughed at or ignored.

Social learning theory argues that gender identification occurs through observing and imitating gender-appropriate behaviour from same-sex models. The theory suggests that children pay more attention to same-sex models, retain their behaviour and then if they are capable of reproducing the behaviour and motivated to do so they will (ARRM). Gender development occurs through imitating gender-appropriate behaviours from same-sex parents, peers and others. For example, a young boy may pay attention to his father fixing a car. He will remember how to do it and reproduce the behaviour when he is motivated to do so.

You need to be able to discuss the nature-nurture debate in the learning approach

Learning theories support the nurture side of the nature-nurture debate. They argue that most of our behaviour is learnt from our environment. However, learning theories accept that we are born with some natural behaviours such as automatic reflexes.

You need to be able to show an understanding of how psychological knowledge had developed over time in relation to learning theories

Learning theories had the most influence on psychological thinking between 1920 and 1950. However, in the 1950s cognitive theories took over. However, many of the principles of learning theories are still used today. For example, behaviour analysts break behaviour down into small components and shape desired behaviour to help those with autism and developmental delays.

You need to be able to discuss issues of social control in relation to learning theories

Learning theories can be used to change and manipulate behaviour and this can be viewed as a form of social control. For example, token economy programmes (TEPs) are used in mental health institutions, schools and prisons to control behaviour. In mental health institutions, patients are rewarded for more adaptive behaviour. For example, anorexic patients are given tokens if they eat well or gain a certain amount of weight each week and these tokens can be exchanged for leisure time or outings. However, if a TEP is the only therapy used it only serves to control their behaviour rather than change it. TEPs may only change behaviour in the short term and learnt behaviour does not transfer easily to the outside world especially if the underlying causes of the disorder have not been dealt with. Token economy programmes are also used with prisoners. Tokens (secondary reinforcers) are given for cooperative and non-aggressive behaviour. Once the prisoners have a certain number of tokens they can exchange them for something they actually wants such as a phone card (a primary reinforcer). However, there are ethical issues with TEPs as staff implementing a token economy programme have a lot of power. It is important that staff do not favour or ignore certain individuals if the programme is to work (the practitioner may have too much influence and power). Therefore, prison staff need to be trained to give tokens fairly and consistently even when there are shift changes.

You need to be able to discuss learning theories and the use of psychological knowledge in society

Learning theories have been applied to many situations. For example, token economy programmes are used in prisons, schools and mental health institutions to improve and change behaviour. Techniques such as flooding and systematic desensitisation have also been used to get rid of phobias.

You need to be able to discuss issues related to socially sensitive research in relation to learning theories

Some treatments based on learning theories are controversial. Aversion Therapy uses classical conditioning to get rid of unwanted behaviours. It works by the association of an unpleasant stimulus with the unwanted behaviour. A paedophile can be conditioned to respond to children with fear rather than sexual arousal by pairing thoughts about children with painful electric shocks. Many people may see this as acceptable as it is performed with the offender's consent and counselling. However, in the past when homosexuality was illegal, aversion therapy was used on homosexual men as an alternative to a prison sentence. This shows how aversion therapy has ethical issues and is open to abuse. Even nowadays, people may only consent to aversion therapy because they feel under pressure to have the treatment and during the treatment they may feel out of control.

Exemplar Exam Question: Discuss issues of social control in relation to treatments and therapies (12 marks)

Student Answer:

Psychological therapies can be used to control people so that they conform to society's norms or for other reasons. When therapies are used to control people rather than to help the individual then this raises ethical issues.
It can be argued that society needs social control so that members of society can work and live together in harmony, without aggression and safely. Society benefits by controlling those with mental health problems and those who commit crimes but but it could be said they benefit too if their lives improve.
Drug therapy is a form of social control and is given to people with mental health problems. For example, schizophrenics are given anti-psychotic drugs to control their symptoms. However, some schizophrenics and their families suggest that the drugs only sedate them rather than help them. There are also many side-effects to taking anti-psychotic drugs. It might be claimed that drugs are a medical 'straitjacket' and are used to control people in a way that seems unethical. Another problem with drug therapy is that it does deal with the underlying causes of mental disorder it just suppresses the symptoms. It could be argued that schizophrenics are given drugs so they live and behave by society's rules and expectations rather than to treat their illness. Another example social control is when drugs such as Ritalin are used to treat children with ADHD. Some argue that as increasing numbers of younger and younger children are being diagnosed with ADHD, it is not a problem with the children but with society. It has been said that Ritalin just slows children down so that parents and teachers can cope with behaviour that might actually be quite normal in young children. Perhaps behaviour management techniques should be taught to parents and teachers so that they can control their children rather than giving the children drugs.

Token economy programmes are used in mental health institutions, schools and prisons to control behaviour and these are a form of social control. In mental health institutions, patients are rewarded for more adaptive behaviour. For example, anorexic patients are given tokens if they eat well or gain a certain amount of weight each week and these tokens can be exchanged for leisure time or outings. However, if a TEP is the only therapy used it only serves to control their behaviour rather than change it. TEPs may only change behaviour in the short term and learnt behaviour does not transfer easily to the outside world especially if the underlying causes of the disorder have not been dealt with. Token economy programmes are also used with prisoners and they are rewarded with tokens for desired behaviour such as compliance and non-aggressive behaviour. The prisoners can then spend the tokens they receive in the way they want to as a sort of shop system is operated in prisons. A problem with using TEPs with prisoners is that it is not effective at reducing recidivism once the criminal has left the prison.

10/12 marks

Commentary: This answer explains issues with social control in relation to drug therapy and token economy programmes well. However, they could have referred to other treatments such as the use of anger management with offenders and cognitive behavioural therapy with mental health patients.

Chapter 4 - Research Methods

You need to be able to describe and evaluate different types of research method used in psychology

Laboratory Experiments

Description:
Laboratory experiments involve manipulating an independent variable and measuring a dependent variable. Extraneous variables are controlled so that a cause and effect relationship can be established.

Evaluation:

Laboratory experiments have standardised procedures, which are easy to replicate so that reliability can be tested. Data from laboratory experiments is quantitative and objective. Therefore, such data is considered scientific. However, laboratory experiments lack ecological validity because they take place in artificial environments and often involve artificial tasks.

Field experiments

Description:

Field experiments are carried out in participants' natural environment. An independent variable is manipulated and a dependent variable is measured. Field experiments often involve a clear procedure and researchers try to control extraneous variables as much as possible so that the study can be tested for reliability.

Evaluation:

Field experiments have greater ecological validity than laboratory experiments as they take place in participants' natural environment. They also have carefully controlled and planned procedures so the study can be repeated. This means that they can be as reliable as laboratory experiments. However, as field experiments take place in the participants' natural environment, not all the extraneous variables can be controlled and the findings might not be reliable despite the researchers' efforts. Field experiments may lack validity as the independent and dependent variables are carefully operationalised.

Natural Experiments

Description:

Natural experiments are carried out in real-life settings. The independent variable occurs naturally but a dependent variable is still measured. It is difficult to establish cause and effect due to lack of control over the independent variable.

Evaluation:

Natural experiments are not reliable as the extraneous variables cannot be controlled due to the natural environment. However, natural experiments have good ecological validity as the participants are in a real-life setting.

Questionnaires

Description

Questionnaires involve written questions to find out about people's views and opinions. They are able to collect data from lots of people as everyone is asked the same questions and can answer them in their own time. Questionnaires can be sent by post, filled in on the internet, given face-to-face or left in a public place for people to pick up. The questions can either be closed or open. Closed questions may involve a Likert type scale or yes/no questions. Open questions ask people explain what they think about a certain topic in their own words. If closed questions are used then quantitative data can be obtained. If open questions are used then qualitative data can be obtained.

Evaluation:

Questionnaires allow data to be gathered from large samples without too much cost. If closed questions are used, the quantitative data can be statistically analysed. It is also easy to compare the data from closed questionnaires as everyone answers the same questions. Questionnaires with closed questions can be easy to replicate. Questionnaires with open questions can collect rich, qualitative data. However, a problem with questionnaires is that people may give socially desirable answers because they want the researchers to think well of them. Participants may also misunderstand the questions and interpret the questions differently. Questions asked beforehand could affect later answers. Questionnaires with closed questions can limit participants' responses, which affects validity. Questionnaires with open questions are subject to interpretation.

Observations

Description:

There are structured laboratory observations and naturalistic observations. Structured laboratory observations involve careful controls and a set-up situation that can be repeated. There is often more than one observer and observations tend to be carried out through a one-way mirror to avoid the researchers' presence affecting participants' behaviour. Naturalistic observations involve observing participants in their natural environment. For example, observing children's behaviour in a playground.

Observations can be overt or covert. Covert observations involve observing a person or group of people without their knowledge. Overt observations involve observing a person or group of people with their knowledge.

Observations can also be participant or non-participant. A participant observation involves the researcher interacting with the person or group of people that they are observing. A non-participant observation involves the researcher observing behaviour from a distance without having any influence or getting involved.

An observation can be carried out by counting the frequency of certain behaviours during a fixed period of time.
Event sampling-when you record every time an event such as a kick occurs
Time sampling-when you record what is happening every set amount of time e.g. every 5 minutes.
Point sampling- The behaviour of just one individual in the group at a time is recorded.
Inter-observer reliability-Comparing the ratings of a number of observers as an individual observer may be biased.This would increase the reliability of the data collected if all the observers agree.

Evaluation:

Researchers may find it difficult to record all the behaviours shown, although event sampling, time sampling and point sampling can help. Video recordings can be used to record participants' behaviour and played back later so that all actions can be noted. It may also be difficult to analyse or interpret all the data collected. Observers often have to be specially trained so that they can record behaviours quickly and to avoid bias.

Participant observations allow researchers to experience the same environment as their participants. However, the researcher's involvement can affect the behaviour of participants. In contrast, non-participant observations allow researchers to observe participants' behaviour more objectively as they are not directly involved in the action. However, if participants are aware they are being observed, they may still change their behaviour.

Covert observations enable researchers to observe participants behave naturally as the participants do not know they are being observed. However, there are ethical issues with observing participants without their consent. They do not have the right to withdraw, they have not given informed consent and there also issues of confidentiality especially if their behaviour has been video-recorded. The British Psychological Society advises that it is only suitable to conduct a covert observation in a place where people might reasonably be expected to be observed by other people such as a shopping centre or other public place. Overt observations do not have as many ethical issues as covert observations. However, when participants know they are being observed they may change their behaviour so that it appears socially desirable. Therefore, overt observations can be less valid.

Interviews

Description:

An interview involves the researcher asking the respondent questions. It may form the basis of a case study or as a follow-up to other research methods. Structured interviews produce quantitative data. All participants are asked the same questions in the same order. They are very similar to questionnaires except questions are read out. An unstructured interview involves an informal or in-depth conversation. Little is planned in advance (perhaps the first couple of questions) and this allows the interviewee to explain answers and introduce new issues. Unstructured interviews obtain rich, qualitative data. A semi-structured interview involves some prepared questions but also some opportunities for interviewees to expand on their answers.

Evaluation:

Unstructured interviews tend to be valid because they allow the interviewer to explore issues that the interviewee wishes to discuss. However, interpretation of participants' responses can be subjective and participants may give socially desirable answers. Certain characteristics about the interviewer such as their dress or manner can also affect replies. Structured interviews are more replicable, and therefore, more reliable.

Content analysis

Description:

A content analysis involves changing qualitative data into quantitative data. This often means tallying how many times certain themes occur within a source such as a newspaper article, magazine article, journal article, radio programme or television programme. The source may be coded or broken down into manageable categories, for example, by words, phrases, sentences or themes. The researcher then analyses the presence and meaning of these categories and draws conclusions. For example, a researcher might tally how often negative or positive comments about daycare occur within two newspaper articles and draw conclusions about how daycare is portrayed in the media.

Evaluation:

As the data comes from secondary sources such as newspaper articles or television programmes, it does not change. Therefore, other researchers can check whether any conclusions are correct or not. The quantitative tallying of themes allows the data to be statistically analysed. There are unlikely to be any ethical issues with a content analysis, as it only involves analysing existing sources. However, the categorising and tallying of themes in a content analysis can be subjective.

Case Studies

Description:

A case study is an in-depth study of one person or one group of people. A number of different techniques are used to gather data. For example, the researcher may observe, interview and carry out a number of experiments on the same person. Triangulation is used to pool data together from the different types of research method and to draw conclusions.

Evaluation:

Case studies are not generalisable as they are carried out on only one person or one group of people who are often unique and not representative of the wider population. It is also difficult to replicate case studies because they involve unique individuals and the interpretation of the observations and interviews is subject to bias. Therefore it is hard to establish reliability in case studies. However, triangulation is used to draw conclusions about the same concept so this improves the reliability of the findings. An advantage of case studies is that they gather rich, detailed information about the individuals using a number of different techniques, so this increases their validity. There can be ethical issues with case studies. Often they involve studying unique individuals who are more vulnerable than normal. Therefore, researchers have to be careful to protect them from psychological distress.

Correlational Techniques

Description:

Correlational studies look for a relationship between two variables. For example, it may look for a relationship between number of hours of violent TV watched and levels of aggression. An example of a positive correlation is: the more hours of violent TV watched, the more aggressive people become. An example of a negative correlation is: the more hours of violent computer games played, the less helpful people are.
Adoption and twin studies are types of correlational study. For example, a twin study might see how strong the relationship is between one twin's IQ and the other twin's IQ.

Evaluation:

Correlational studies can demonstrate a relationship between two variables, which was not noticed before. They can also be used to look for relationships between variables that cannot be investigated by other means. For example, researchers can look to see whether there is a relationship between parents having low expectations of their children and the children's later academic performance. Manipulating such variables would be unethical. However, correlational studies cannot establish cause and effect relationships. A third factor may affect both variables under investigation. For example, although a correlational study might show a relationship between the number of hours of violent TV watched and levels of aggression, we cannot be certain that the violent TV programmes led to the aggression. It may be that children who watch violent TV programmes are naturally more aggressive and so seek such programmes out.

Thematic Analysis

Description:

A thematic analysis can be used to analyse different types of data, from media articles to transcripts of focus groups or interviews. It is suitable for analysing people's experiences, opinions and perceptions. It can also be used to look at how different issues and concepts are constructed or represented. There are a number of stages in carrying out a thematic analysis: 1) The researcher familiarises themselves with the data by reading it several times; 2) Codes are generated for important features of the data; 3) The researcher looks for themes by examining the codes and collated data to identify broader patterns of meaning (potential themes); 4) The themes are reviewed by checking them against what people have said. At this stage, themes may be refined or discarded; 5) Themes are named and a detailed analysis of each theme is carried out; 6) Finally, the themes are written up with quotes from the data collected. The analysis is linked to existing theories.

Evaluation:

A thematic analysis can be used for a wide range of research questions. Rich, detailed data can be obtained, which can lead to a deeper insight into people's experiences, opinions and representations. However, thematic analyses are open to interpretation and hence subjective. They can be hard to replicate and so they have problems with reliability.

Longitudinal Studies

Description:

Longitudinal studies involve studying the same person or group of people over a long period of time. For example, researchers might look at the impact of childcare on children's cognitive, social and emotional development over a 10 year period.

Evaluation:

An advantage of longitudinal studies is that they allow researchers to follow the development and progress of an individual or group of individuals over time. There are also less likely to be participant variables as the same people are used and their progress can be tracked. However, longitudinal studies can be expensive. Furthermore, erosion of the sample (participants dropping out of the study) may cause bias.

Cross-sectional Studies

Description:

Cross-sectional studies involve gathering data at one moment in time from different groups of people so that one group is compared with another group on the same characteristics, behaviour or task i.e. a cross-sectional study might compare anorexic patients of different ages at the same time.

Evaluation:

Cross-sectional designs tend to be cheaper, quicker and more practical than longitudinal designs as participants are tested at one moment in time. However, as different participants are used in the conditions, participant variables can affect results.

Meta-analyses

Description:

Meta-analyses look at the findings of a number of different studies and draw conclusions. For example, a meta-analysis might investigate whether the media influences aggressive behaviour by analysing the results of 50 studies.

Evaluation:

Meta-analyses can be carried out quickly at little cost. They are useful when there is a lot of research on a specific topic such as the effect of the media on aggressive behaviour and conclusions need to be drawn. However, not all studies are equally reliable and valid and some studies may be included in a meta-analysis that distort results.

You need to be able to define quantitative and qualitative and give general strengths and weaknesses of both (including issues of reliability and validity.

Quantitative data is numerical data. Quantitative research e.g. laboratory experiments tend to use large samples of people or animals so that results can be generalised to the wider population. Statistical tests can be done on quantitative data to see how far the results are likely to be due to chance. If a quantitative research is repeated, often the same data will be found. This shows that quantitative data is reliable. However, the careful operationalising of variables in quantitative research means that real life events and interactions are not being measured (lack of validity).

Qualitative data is descriptive and often takes into account people's views and opinions. It can be gathered in natural situations so it is valid. However, qualitative data is harder to replicate and can lack reliability.

You need to know which research methods produce quantitative data and to be able to describe them.

Experiments, questionnaires with closed questions and structured interviews are good sources of quantitative data.
Questionnaires with closed questions consist of a list of pre-set questions that a participant answers usually involving yes/no or applying a scale.

Experiments are controlled studies often carries out in controlled conditions. An IV is manipulated and then a DV measured as a result. Objectivity is aimed for, hence the controls.

Structured interviews have set questions and there is an interviewer who asks questions.

You need to know which research methods produce qualitative data.

Case studies, unstructured interviews, clinical interviews and questionnaires with open questions produce qualitative data.

Case studies aim for an in-depth study of one individual or group. They gather information from many sources using more than one means of gathering data.

Unstructured interviews may begin with an aim and an idea of what questions are to be answered. They do not have set questions. The interviewer can explore areas that come up.

Clinical interviews involve an analyst listening to a client and using techniques such as free association and dream analysis. The aim is to uncover unconscious thoughts.

Questionnaires with open questions have preset questions but participants are able to express their views and opinions freely. There is no scale.

You need to be able to compare research methods.

If you are asked to compare research methods, you should consider the following:

Does the research method collect quantitative or qualitative data? If the research method collects quantitative data then it can be statistically analysed and is more objective. If the research method collects qualitative data it is usually more detailed and richer. However, the data is likely to be subjective.

Does the research method use primary or secondary data?

Does the research method give reliable data? Are studies using this research method easy to repeat?

Does the research method give valid data? Do studies using this research method collect rich, detailed in-depth data? Are studies using this research method carried out in participants' natural environment?

Does the research method require more than one researcher to carry out the study? For example, observations require more than one observer to establish inter-observer reliability.

How do the research methods gather data? Is any counting involved? Is any description involved?

Exam tip: When comparing, do not just describe each research method in turn. Instead, describe how the research methods are similar or different.

Exemplar exam question: A researcher wants to investigate how students feel about the way universities recruit applicants. The researcher decided to conduct a survey.

a) Explain how the researcher might design and carry out the survey. (6 marks)

Student answer:

The researcher could carry out a structured questionnaire with closed questions and a Likert scale to find out about students' opinions on the application procedure for university. Once the researcher has come up with their questions, they could test their questions on a few participants to see whether they make sense in a pilot study. They can then use any feedback from participants to adjust their questions. The questionnaire could then be set up on a website such as Survey Monkey so that participants can complete it in online in their own time. The researcher could then approach schools and ask them whether they would pass on the website address for their online questionnaire to students applying for university. The schools could be told that they will be given a copy of the research findings, which they may find useful. However, participants would need to know that their anonymity would be protected; otherwise they may be worried about being honest. Once a certain time period has elapsed such as 2 months the questionnaire could be closed.

Commentary:

This student has applied their understanding of questionnaires to the scenario well. However, they could have discussed how they decided on which questions to ask. It would have been necessary to conduct some preliminary research to decide what concerns students have about the university application process. There should also have been some discussion about sample size; a few hundred responses are required for the sample to be representative. Another point that could have been covered is how the data would be analysed. Quantitative data from a structured questionnaire using a Likert scale can be analysed statistically.

b) The researcher recruits her sample by sending leaflets round to school sixth forms asking students to take part. Explain the strengths and weaknesses of recruiting a sample in this way. (4 marks)

Student answer:

The sample was a volunteer sample. Participants who have volunteered for a study are less likely to drop out as they have agreed to take part in the study. However, they are also unlikely to be representative of the wider population as only certain people will volunteer to take part. Volunteers are often more helpful than the wider population and this can lead to demand characteristics.

Commentary:

This student could have expanded their point about why volunteers are unrepresentative of the wider population. Volunteers often have more time, are more willing to please and are more helpful than the wider population. An advantage of volunteer samples is that it can be quick and cheap to recruit volunteers as the researchers do not have to be careful about how they select participants unlike a quota sample.

Printed in Great Britain
by Amazon